## NOTES

Both metric and imperial measurements have been given in all recipes. Use one set of measurements only, and not a mixture of both.

- Standard level spoon measurements are used in all recipes.
- 1 tablespoon = one 15 ml spoon
- 1 teaspoon = one 5 ml spoon
- All eggs used in the recipes are medium.

Ovens should be preheated to the specified temperature – if using a fan-assisted oven, follow the manufacturer's instructions for adjusting the time and the temperature.

This book includes dishes made with nuts and nut derivatives. It is advisable for those with known allergic reactions to nuts and nut derivatives and those who may be potentially vulnerable to these allergies, such as pregnant and nursing mothers, invalids, the elderly, babies and children, to avoid foods made with nuts. It is also prudent to check the labels of pre-prepared ingredients for the possible inclusion of nut derivatives.

Children should be supervised by an adult at all times when cooking or baking. The tasks that can be performed at a particular age or stage in their development will differ from child to child.

An Hachette UK Company
www.hachette.co.uk

First published in Great Britain in 2007 by Hamlyn, a division of Octopus Publishing Group Limited, Endeavour House, 189 Shaftesbury Avenue, London WC2H 8JY
www.octopusbooks.co.uk

Revised edition published in 2014.

Becky Johnson asserts the moral right to be identified as the author of this work.

ISBN 978-0-600-62912-2

A CIP catalogue record for this book is available from the British Library.

Printed and bound in China.

10 9 8 7 6 5 4 3 2 1

# my *first* Baking Book

## 50 RECIPES FOR KIDS TO MAKE AND EAT!

### BECKY JOHNSON

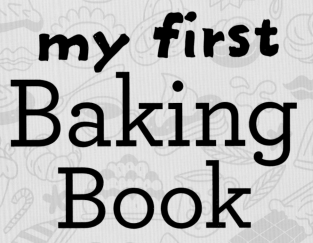

# Contents

# Introduction

Whoever said never to work with children or animals has obviously not tried baking with little ones as it is a joy to cook with even the tiniest of tots. OK, so it may get a little messy but the results are worth it. Children's energy and enthusiasm for cooking are a real inspiration, and any doubts that a few of the trickier tasks like piping, kneading or rubbing in are beyond their young years are often dispelled by displays of earnest concentration, determination and exuberant completion of the task in hand. That they are then able to eat the results of their labour is invariably met with wonder and joy.

Children like to feel that they contribute to family life. They want to be helpful and do what they see you doing. Baking is one way that they can produce real results, ones that everyone can enjoy and appreciate. My seven-year-old daughter is genuinely excited by other people's birthdays now as she insists on making them a cake. This is always received with rapturous delight, making her rightly proud. This book is full of child-friendly ideas for food that you and your little ones can bake together, and all the recipes have been tested on children. A family baking session is a lovely way to spend time together. In this book you'll find ideas for a quick lunch or a teatime cake through to edible Christmas decorations and party treats. Together you can make the food for a picnic or their lunch box, delicious gifts for friends and relatives and irresistible snacks for the cookie jar or cake tin.

**ADDITIVE-FREE FOOD** Baking at home also gives control back to us parents over what our children eat. The kids can still enjoy sweet treats but without the long list of additives most of us know little about and fear may harm their growing bodies.

Instead of giving your children a shop-bought cake, open their young minds to the wonderful variety of textures, smells and tastes of home baking. Show them where their food comes from and how they can combine different ingredients to make yummy biscuits, cakes and pastries. With a little encouragement, a lifelong interest in real food and home cooking may easily be sparked at this tender age.

**BE RELAXED** A child's first baking experience needs to be fun. All the recipes in this book are easy and quite quick. They don't require long attention spans but be prepared to step in if your child is wavering before completing the whole tray of cookies! I found that my daughter was always happy to sit and lick out the bowl, or 'help' with the washing up in a sink full of bubbles, while I finished off the recipe.

The important thing when cooking with little children is to allow lots of time – children hate being hurried – and not to worry too much about the look of the results! It's the time spent creating something together that's important.

**LEARNING IS FUN** Children learn a huge amount from cooking without even really realizing. Firstly, there's the exposure to cookbooks full of recipes. From these they learn that the written word provides information that can be used to make things. They also see photos of other children doing things they will then want to try themselves. Secondly, there's the coordination that is required to measure out ingredients, to mix, spoon out, beat and spread. Next, weighing and measuring things introduce children to the concepts of numbers, weights, accuracy and volume. Lastly, there's the chemistry involved in the baking itself – the transforming effect of heat on food.

**ENCOURAGING INDEPENDENCE** Because cooking is an activity that uses all of the senses, it is totally absorbing for children. It gives them a sense of achievement and confidence as they try new actions by themselves. As they become older and more capable, your children will be able to make their favourite foods by themselves, and developing a familiarity with food and cooking at a young age may give them the confidence to be more creative in the kitchen in later life. We live in an age where many parents don't know how to cook, and rely heavily on quick convenience foods and pre-prepared meals. Encouraging your children to cook for themselves and learn how to transform sets of ingredients into cakes, biscuits and eventually casseroles and roast dinners can only be a good thing for them in adulthood and will hopefully encourage them to pass these skills on to their own children in time.

## SHOPPING FOR INGREDIENTS

Not only do children learn about food and cooking when in the kitchen, but taking them shopping for the ingredients you're going to use is a useful learning experience, too. Whether they're sitting in the trolley, or walking along beside you in the supermarket, involve your children in the food shopping process. Teach them how to locate items along the aisles, get them to help you track down specific ingredients and explain their uses and their origin if possible. It all helps spark children's interest and may even encourage fussy eaters to try unfamiliar foods once back at home.

## WHAT CAN YOUR CHILD DO?

Children can – and indeed like to – help you in the kitchen from the time they are old enough to stand on a chair and reach the worktop. Covering their hands with yours and letting them think they are cutting butter or spreading icing gives them a huge thrill and costs you nothing but patience. Even the smallest child should be able to use a cookie cutter to cut shapes out of dough. Children develop at different rates but between the ages of three and six you'll find they can wash fruits and vegetables for you, stir ingredients in a bowl and, under direction, add ingredients to the bowl.

Over-sixes will be able to use measuring spoons, measure liquids into a jug and beat ingredients with a whisk.

Recipe steps that young children should find particularly easy to carry out are marked with this splash icon. Adult supervision is recommended at all times.

## TIPS FOR KNEADING DOUGH
The best bit of kneading is that it doesn't really need to be done in any specific way so you can throw the dough down on the table and punch it, pull it and twist it. Children are very good at kneading dough, but if they need some instruction, tell them to grab the side of the dough nearest to them and, keeping hold of it, push the other side of the dough down and away from them with the palm of their hand. Then lift the far edge up and over into the centre. Now give the dough a quarter turn and knead again as before. Do this for at least 10 minutes or until the dough becomes smooth textured, elastic and no longer sticky. Children can become tired kneading dough, so do be prepared to step in and finish off the job.

## GETTING STARTED
First choose your recipe, bearing in mind the age and ability of your little one. Remember that cooking with a little one takes much longer than cooking on your own, so make sure you have plenty of time to complete the recipe. Collect together all the necessary ingredients and equipment before you start so you can check you've got what you need. It's infuriating to have to abandon a recipe halfway through cooking because you're missing an ingredient you thought you had. It will also cause intense disappointment on the part of your assistant chef!

# WHAT YOU'LL NEED

You don't have to buy any special equipment in order to bake with your children but certain items will make life easier for them so may mean they enjoy the baking experience more.

**STEP-UP STOOL** It's worth investing in a child's step-up stool or a child-sized chair so that your child can see above the worktop and/or have a low table that they can work on. Alternatively, they could sit on a clean floor or on a plastic sheet or tablecloth.

**APRON** A little apron is a treat for small cooks. A wipe-clean one will make it particularly easy to avoid splashes and keep your little one clean. A cheaper alternative is to use an old shirt (check out the charity shop) or even a raincoat!

**DIGITAL WEIGHING SCALES** These are the easiest type of scales for children to use as the figures are clear and easy to read, and it's easier for children to match them exactly to what's given in the recipe book.

**SMALL WOODEN SPOON** A child-sized wooden spoon makes beating and mixing much easier for very little ones.

**A SET OF MEASURING SPOONS** These are very useful for accurately measuring ingredients in whole and fractions of teaspoons and tablespoons. Fill the spoons level – a rounded measure could end up almost doubling the amount of ingredient required! Try not to use everyday spoons as their designs, depths and shapes vary.

**PLASTIC MEASURING JUGS AND BOWLS** Plastic equipment is obviously better than glass for children to use, in case of clumsy hands.

## SAFETY FIRST

Children must always be supervised in the kitchen. Teach them basic hygiene rules from an early age, and tell them about the potential dangers posed by hot ovens, full saucepans and sharp knives and scissors.

**HYGIENE** Always wash hands before starting to cook and make sure surfaces are clean. Tie back long hair and put on an apron or coverall.

**OVENS AND HOBS** Take special care when opening oven doors in front of expectant little ones and make sure they stand well back so they don't get blasted by very hot air. Always use oven gloves. Also be especially wary of recently turned off but still very hot hobs. Use the back rings of the hob when working with small children so there's no temptation for them to grab saucepan handles from below to see what's cooking.

**SHARP KNIVES** It's great to involve young children in the clearing-up process – to them it's just as much fun as the cooking and you can establish good working practices from the start. But make it a rule never to place any sharp knives or food processor blades in the sink, where they can easily be hidden by soap bubbles. Instead, rinse them as you go and place them straight back on to the knife rack or into a drawer, well out of harm's way.

## STORAGE

If you don't eat them all within hours of baking them, most of the cakes and biscuits in this book will keep for 2–3 days in an airtight container, such as a cake tin or cookie jar. If you want to prepare in advance or decide you only want to finish off half the quantity you have made, uncooked biscuit dough and un-iced cakes can be placed in plastic food storage bags and frozen for up to a month.

# A Piece of Cake

# Lemon sandcastles

**MAKES** 6  **PREP TIME** 15 minutes  **COOKING TIME** 20 minutes

**Planted with cocktail stick flags, these little lemon cakes look like sandcastles and even have an authentic 'gritty' texture from the polenta.**

## Equipment

6 dariole moulds (or 6-cup muffin tin) • nonstick baking paper • pencil • scissors • kitchen paper • large mixing bowl • wooden spoon • small mixing bowl • sieve • dessertspoon • baking sheet • knife • cooling rack • teaspoon • medium mixing bowl

## Ingredients

- 100 g (3½ oz) butter or margarine, softened, plus extra for greasing
- 100 g (3½ oz) caster sugar
- 2 eggs
- 125 g (4 oz) self-raising flour
- 50 g (2 oz) polenta (ordinary or quickcook variety)
- grated rind of a lemon
- 2 tablespoons natural yogurt

FOR THE ICING
- 200 g (7 oz) icing sugar, sifted
- juice of ½ an unwaxed lemon
- pinch of saffron (strands or powdered) soaked in 1 tablespoon boiling water
- flags, sweets or cake decorations, to decorate

**1** Set the oven to 180°C (350°F), Gas Mark 4. To line the bottom of the dariole moulds, place them on a piece of nonstick baking paper and allow your child to draw around them with a pencil. Then, if the little hands have mastered scissors, cut around the circles and place one in the bottom of each mould.

**2** Using kitchen paper, smear some butter or margarine around the sides of the moulds so that the cakes won't stick. If you don't have dariole moulds, use a muffin tin and prepare the same way.

**3** After helping you measure out the butter or margarine and the sugar into a large mixing bowl, let your child do the mixing with a wooden spoon until really creamy.

**4** Break the eggs carefully into a small bowl and add them to the large bowl one at a time, stirring in well. Finally, sift in the flour, add all the other ingredients and stir together until you have a smooth mixture.

**5** Help your child to use a dessertspoon to spoon the mixture into the prepared tins until they are about two-thirds full.

**6** Place all the moulds together on a baking sheet and bake for 20 minutes or until golden on top.

**7** Slide a knife around the edge of the tins to loosen the cakes, tip on to a cooling rack and leave until cool.

**8** While the cakes are cooling, your child can mix together the ingredients to make the icing. Drizzle over the cakes with a teaspoon, then decorate with flags, sweets or cake decorations.

**DRIZZLE THE ICING**
USING A TEASPOON

# Yummy stars

**MAKES** 15  **PREP TIME** 20 minutes  **COOKING TIME** 35 minutes

### Dark, moist gingerbread cut into stars and drizzled with a bright white glacé icing and sugar stars or silver baubles.

## Equipment

large baking tin, 30 cm (12 inches) square • nonstick baking paper • pencil • scissors • small saucepan • large mixing bowl • wooden spoon or hand-held electric whisk • sieve • spatula • thin wooden or metal skewer • star-shaped cutter • dessertspoon • small mixing bowl • teaspoon

## Ingredients

- 1 tablespoon black treacle
- 150 g (5 oz) butter or margarine, softened
- 150 g (5 oz) dark brown sugar
- 1 egg
- 300 g (10 oz) self-raising flour
- 2 teaspoons ground ginger
- 150 ml (¼ pint) natural yogurt
FOR THE ICING
- 1 tablespoon lemon juice (or water)
- 200 g (7 oz) icing sugar, sifted
- 1 tablespoon warm water
- edible silver and green baubles, to decorate

**1** Place the baking tin on a sheet of baking paper and have your child draw around it with a pencil.

**2** Cut out the square and place it in the bottom of the tin. Set the oven to 150°C (300°F), Gas Mark 2. Put the treacle in a small saucepan and heat gently.

**3** Put the butter and sugar in the large mixing bowl and help your child to beat them together until creamy.

**4** Add the treacle and egg and stir to combine. Sift in the flour and stir in the ginger and yogurt. Scrape into the prepared tin with a spatula and bake for 30 minutes or until a skewer inserted in the middle comes out clean.

**5** Leave the cake in the tin to cool, then tip out and, using a star cutter, help your child to cut the cake into 15 star shapes. Eat the trimmings!

**6** Meanwhile, make the icing by stirring together the ingredients in a small bowl. Drizzle the icing over the stars with a teaspoon and then decorate with silver and green baubles.

# Rock buns

**MAKES** 12   **PREP TIME** 15 minutes   **COOKING TIME** 15–20 minutes

contrary to their name, these little
buns are soft and sweet, but they do look
rather like rugged rocks.

## Equipment

nonstick baking paper • scissors •
2 large baking sheets • large mixing
bowl • sieve • wooden spoon •
dessertspoon • cooling rack

## Ingredients

- 100 g (3½ oz) butter, softened
- 225 g (7½ oz) self-raising flour
- ½ teaspoon ground cinnamon
  (optional)
- grated rind of an orange
- 100 g (3½ oz) demerara sugar,
  plus extra for sprinkling
- 100 g (3½ oz) mixed dried fruit
  (if your child is not keen on the
  shop-bought mixes, you can make
  your own by chopping citrus peel,
  dried apricots and glacé cherries)
- 1 egg, beaten
- drop of milk (optional)

**1** Help your child to cut large pieces of the baking paper to fit the baking sheets while you set the oven to 200°C (400°F), Gas Mark 6.

**2** Put the butter into a large bowl, sift in the flour and cinnamon, if using, and tell your child to rub the flour and butter together with their hands until the butter is all broken up and covered in flour and the mixture resembles breadcrumbs.

**3** Add the orange rind, sugar, fruit and egg and stir it all together with a wooden spoon (this stage is too sticky for hands to manage). Add a little milk if the mixture is too crumbly.

**4** Use a dessertspoon to put about 12 untidy mounds of the mixture on to the baking sheets.

**5** Sprinkle the tops of the buns with a little more demerara sugar, then bake for 15–20 minutes or until golden brown on the edges.

**6** Remove the buns from the oven and allow to cool for 15 minutes on the trays, then transfer to a cooling rack.

# Blueberry muffins

MAKES 12   PREP TIME 15 minutes   COOKING TIME 20 minutes

Quick and easy, these ingredients could be
measured out, placed in two separate bowls the night
before, then put together and baked for a special
breakfast - a Mother's Day treat perhaps.

## Equipment

12 paper muffin cases • 12-cup
muffin tin • 2 large mixing bowls •
sieve • wooden spoon • dessertspoon
• cooling rack

## Ingredients

- 200 g (7 oz) self-raising flour
- ½ teaspoon bicarbonate of soda
- 100 g (3½ oz) soft light brown
  sugar, plus extra for sprinkling
- 100 g (3½ oz) butter, melted
- 100 ml (3½ fl oz) natural yogurt
- 100 ml (3½ fl oz) milk
- 1 egg, beaten
- 200 g (7 oz) blueberries
- 1 dessert apple, cored, peeled
  and diced quite small

**1** Show your child how to put the paper cases into the
muffin tin while you set the oven to 200°C (400°F),
Gas Mark 6.

**2** Divide the ingredients into 2 large mixing bowls: all
the dry ingredients (sifted flour, bicarbonate of soda
and sugar) in one bowl and all the wet (melted butter,
yogurt, milk, egg, blueberries and apple) in another.

**3** Ask your child to stir the ingredients in their separate
bowls until well mixed.

**4** Help your child pour the wet ingredients into the dry.
It is important to mix quickly and minimally – as with
all muffins, it's best to have a lumpy mixture that will
be soft and rise rather than a well-mixed one that
will not rise and be tough.

**5** Quickly spoon the mixture into the prepared cases so
that each is about three-quarters full. Have your child
sprinkle each with a little more of the sugar. Bake for
20 minutes or until risen and golden.

**6** Remove the muffins from the oven and let them cool
a little in the tin before transferring to a cooling rack.
Eat warm or cold.

# Lamingtons

**MAKES** 12   **PREP TIME** 20 minutes   **COOKING TIME** 15–20 minutes

**As Australian as kangaroos, these jam-filled sponge cakes taste exceedingly good and are fun and messy to make!**

## Equipment

2 x 1 kg (2 lb) loaf tins • nonstick baking paper • large mixing bowl • wooden spoon, fork or hand-held electric whisk • sieve • dessertspoon • cooling rack • medium mixing bowl • small bowl • saucer • large serrated knife • palette knife • board or plate

## Ingredients

- 100 g (3½ oz) butter or margarine, softened, plus extra for greasing
- 100 g (3½ oz) caster sugar
- 2 eggs
- 200 g (7 oz) self-raising flour
- 1 teaspoon vanilla essence
- about 3 tablespoons milk

FOR THE ICING
- 50 g (2 oz) butter or margarine, softened
- 150 g (5 oz) icing sugar, sifted
- 1 tablespoon cocoa powder
- 2–3 tablespoons pre-boiled water
- 50–75 g (2–3 oz) desiccated coconut
- 1–2 tablespoons milk (optional)

FOR THE FILLING
- 4 tablespoons raspberry or strawberry jam

**1** Set the oven to 180°C (350°F), Gas Mark 4, and grease and line the loaf tins with nonstick baking paper.

**2** Put the butter and sugar in a large mixing bowl and, using a wooden spoon, fork or electric beater, mash them together until light and creamy.

**3** Beat in the eggs one at a time. Sift in the flour, add the vanilla essence and just enough milk to combine to a soft dropping consistency.

**4** Spoon into the prepared tins and smooth the top. Bake for 15–20 minutes or until golden brown and springy to the touch. Remove from the tin and cool on a cooling rack.

**5** Meanwhile, make the icing. Beat the butter and sugar together in a mixing bowl until light and creamy. In a separate small bowl, mix the cocoa and pre-boiled warm water together and then add to the butter mix and beat until smooth.

**6** Tip the desiccated coconut into a saucer. Slice the cakes in half crossways through the middle and spread the bases with jam. Replace the tops and cut each cake into 6 equal-sized squares.

**7** Dip all sides of the squares first into the chocolate icing and then into the coconut. Set on to a board or plate to dry completely before serving (if towards the end the icing becomes too thick, simply thin it down with a spoonful or two of milk).

# Banana muffins

**MAKES** 6   **PREP TIME** 15 minutes   **COOKING TIME** 25–30 minutes

### A great recipe for little ones to make as the secret to a good muffin is not to mix it too well. Lumpy is good!

## Equipment

6 paper muffin cases • 6-cup muffin tin • small saucepan • fork • small mixing bowl • sieve • large mixing bowl • wooden spoon • dessertspoon • cooling rack • teaspoon

## Ingredients

- 25 g (1 oz) butter
- 2 tablespoons runny honey
- 2 tablespoons milk
- 2 large very ripe bananas
- 150 g (5 oz) self-raising flour
- ½ teaspoon bicarbonate of soda

FOR THE ICING

- 175 g (6 oz) icing sugar
- 1 teaspoon caramel sauce
- 2–3 tablespoons pre-boiled warm water
- dried banana chips, to decorate

**1** Ask your child to place the paper cases in the tin while you set the oven to 180°C (350°F), Gas Mark 4.

**2** Put the butter, honey and milk in the small pan and place on a low heat until melted.

**3** Show your child how to mash the bananas with a fork in the small bowl. Sift the flour and bicarbonate of soda into a large bowl and mix together.

**4** Pour the melted butter mixture into the mashed bananas and mix, then tip into the flour and mix together with a wooden spoon. At this stage tell your child not to overmix – just a couple of stirs will do or the muffins will be tough and flat.

**5** Without delay, spoon the mixture into the muffin cases so that each is about two-thirds full. Bake for 20–25 minutes until risen and golden.

**6** Remove from the oven and allow to cool in the tin for 5 minutes, then transfer the muffins in their cases to a cooling rack.

**7** While the muffins are cooling, make the caramel icing. Sift the icing sugar into a bowl, add the caramel sauce and mix together with enough of the pre-boiled warm water to make a thick but spoonable icing.

**8** When cool, ask your child to blob the icing on top of each muffin with a teaspoon and let it run. Stick a banana chip to the wet icing to decorate.

**MASH THE BANANAS**
USING A FORK

# Rainbow buns

**MAKES** 24 (or 12)   **PREP TIME** 20 minutes   **COOKING TIME** 10–15 minutes

## These little orange-scented buns are iced and dipped in hundreds and thousands.

### Equipment

24 small cake cases or 12 cup cake cases • 24- or 12-cup bun tray • large mixing bowl • wooden spoon • sieve • teaspoon • cooling rack • medium mixing bowl • dessertspoon • saucer

### Ingredients

- 50 g (2 oz) butter or margarine, softened
- 50 g (2 oz) caster sugar
- grated rind of an unwaxed orange
- few drops of vanilla essence
- 1 egg
- 50 g (2 oz) self-raising flour

FOR THE ICING

- 175 g (6 oz) icing sugar
- 2 tablespoons orange juice
- hundreds and thousands or other cake decorations, to decorate

**1** Show your child how to place the cake cases in the bun tray while you set the oven to 180°C (350°F), Gas Mark 4.

**2** Put the butter, sugar, orange rind and vanilla essence into the large mixing bowl and help your child beat them together until creamy.

**3** Add the egg and beat the mixture again, then sift in the flour and stir it in. Spoon the mixture into the cake cases with a teaspoon so they are three-quarters full.

**4** Bake the buns for 10–15 minutes or until they are risen and golden. Remove from the oven and allow to cool for a few minutes before transferring to a cooling rack and letting them cool completely.

**5** Meanwhile, make the icing by sifting the icing sugar into a bowl and stirring in the orange juice.

**6** When the cakes are cool, drizzle the icing over them with a teaspoon or dip them into the icing to cover. Pour the hundreds and thousands into a saucer and dip in the iced cakes. Leave to set.

**PLACE ON A PLATE**
AND LEAVE TO SET

# Flower fairy cakes

**MAKES** 12 **PREP TIME** 10 minutes **COOKING TIME** 15–20 minutes

### children love to ice and decorate these pretty, light-as-fairies buns.

## Equipment

12 paper muffin cases • 12-cup muffin tin • food processor (or mixing bowl and wooden spoon) • dessertspoon • cooling rack • sharp knife • small bowls for colouring the icing • teaspoons

## Ingredients

- 125 g (4 oz) butter or margarine, softened
- 125 g (4 oz) caster sugar
- 2 eggs
- 125 g (4 oz) self-raising flour
- few drops of vanilla essence
- 2 tablespoons milk

FOR THE ICING

- 500 g (1 lb) pack instant royal icing
- food colouring (optional: one or more colours, as liked)
- sugar or rice paper flowers or other cake decorations, to decorate

**1** Ask your child to put the paper cases in the muffin tin while you set the oven to 180°C (350°F), Gas Mark 4.

**2** If you have a food processor, put all the ingredients except the milk into it and mix until smooth, then add the milk a little at a time down the funnel of the food processor until you have a mixture that is a soft, dropping consistency. Alternatively, follow steps 2–3 of the Lamington recipe on page 23 for the manual method.

**3** Help your child to spoon the mixture into the paper muffin cases.

**4** Bake the cakes for 15–20 minutes or until they are golden and springy to the touch. Allow to cool for a few minutes in the tin, then transfer to a cooling rack. When cool, slice off the pointy tops with a sharp knife.

**5** Make up the royal icing as directed on the pack and divide into small bowls, one for each choice of colour.

**6** To colour the royal icing if liked, first cover any porous work surface with a plastic cloth or newspaper, or work on a metal draining board. Pour a few drops of colouring into the lid of the bottle, then ask your child to add the colouring to the first bowl of icing drop by drop. Add different colouring to the other bowls of icing if you like.

**7** Mix the icing well and let your child spoon the icing on to the cakes and decorate to their taste.

# Mud pies

This recipe is a little bit tricky in that it needs a lot of whisking, but it's worth the effort for the rich, gooey mud mixture and resulting irresistible pies.

## Equipment

12 paper muffin cases • 12-cup muffin tin • small saucepan • medium heatproof bowl • wooden spoon • large mixing bowl, preferably with a pouring lip • hand-held electric whisk (or food processor with whisk attachment) • sieve • large metal spoon • cooling rack • tea strainer or small sieve

## Ingredients

- 200 g (7 oz) plain chocolate, broken into small pieces
- 200 g (7 oz) butter
- 3 eggs
- 75 g (3 oz) caster sugar
- 100 g (3½ oz) self-raising flour
- 2 tablespoons cocoa powder or icing sugar, to decorate (optional)

**1** Ask your child to put the paper cases in the muffin tin while you set the oven to 160°C (325°F), Gas Mark 3.

**2** Boil the kettle and pour 5 cm (2 inches) of water into the small saucepan and set it over a low heat so that the water is simmering.

**3** Put the chocolate pieces and butter in the heatproof bowl and place over the simmering water in the saucepan until melted, then stir together gently.

**4** Put the eggs and sugar in the large mixing bowl and help your child to beat with the electric whisk for a full 5 minutes until very light and foamy. Alternatively, this could be done more easily in a food processor with a whisk attachment.

**5** Have your child sift the flour into the egg foam. Add the chocolate mixture and show them how to fold them together with a large metal spoon, being careful not to knock all the air out of the mixture.

**6** Help them to pour or spoon the 'mud' into the muffin cases so that each is about half full, then bake for 15 minutes.

**7** When they are cooked, remove them from the oven and allow to cool for 5–10 minutes in the tin before transferring them to a cooling rack.

**8** If you wish, your child can put a tablespoon or so of cocoa powder or icing sugar into a tea strainer or small sieve and dust the cakes to decorate.

# Chocolate teddies

**MAKES** 12 **PREP TIME** 20 minutes **COOKING TIME** 10–15 minutes

The easiest one-bowl bun mixture made with milk and white chocolate chips. We've decorated them as teddies but let your child use their own decorative ideas.

## Equipment

12 cup cake cases • 12-cup bun tray • large mixing bowl • wooden spoon • sieve • dessertspoon • cooling rack • medium mixing bowl • fork

## Ingredients

- 100 g (3½ oz) butter, softened
- 100 g (3½ oz) caster sugar
- few drops of vanilla essence
- 2 eggs
- 100 g (3½ oz) self-raising flour
- 50 g (2 oz) milk chocolate drops
- 50 g (2 oz) white chocolate drops

FOR THE ICING
- 150 g (5 oz) icing sugar
- 2 tablespoons cocoa powder
- 50 g (2 oz) butter, softened
- white and milk chocolate buttons or drops, to decorate

**1** Show your child how to place the paper cases in the bun tray while you set the oven to 180°C (350°F), Gas Mark 4.

**2** Put the butter, sugar and vanilla essence in the mixing bowl and help your child beat them together until creamy.

**3** Add the eggs and beat the mixture again, then sift in the flour and stir it in. Finally, stir in the chocolate drops. Spoon the mixture into the cake cases with a dessertspoon so that they are three-quarters full.

**4** Bake for 10–15 minutes or until risen and golden. Remove from the oven and allow to cool for a few minutes before transferring to a cooling rack and letting cool completely.

**5** Meanwhile, make the chocolate icing by sifting the icing sugar and cocoa into a bowl, adding the butter, then beating the ingredients together until smooth.

**6** When the cakes are cool, spread them with the icing. Use a fork to make the icing look like fur and then decorate them, making eyes, ears and a nose.

**USE CHOCOLATE BUTTONS**
TO MAKE A FACE ON EACH CAKE

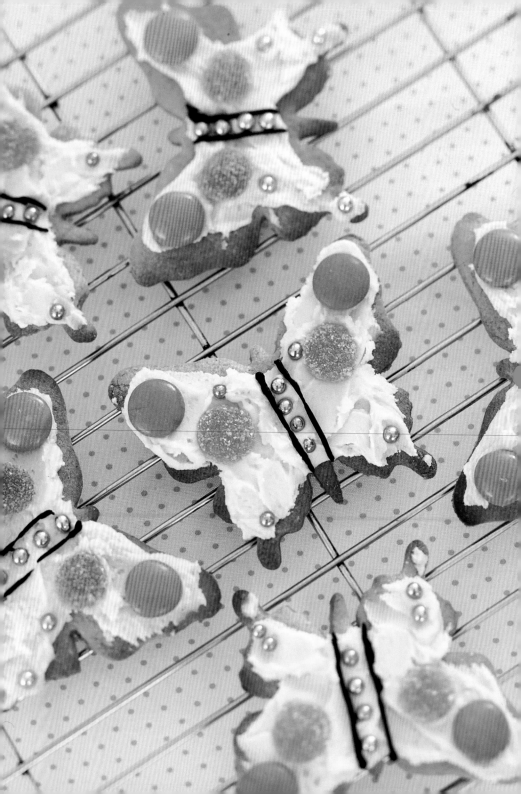

# Cute Cookies

# Choc-chip cookies

**MAKES** about 24   **PREP TIME** 10 minutes   **COOKING TIME** 10–15 minutes

### These chunky, chocolate-chip-laden cookies are quick, easy and fun to make.

## Equipment

nonstick baking paper • scissors • 2 large baking sheets • large mixing bowl • hand-held electric whisk or wooden spoon • sieve • teaspoon • fish slice or palette knife • cooling rack

## Ingredients

- 100 g (3½ oz) butter or margarine, softened
- 100 g (3½ oz) soft light brown sugar
- 1 egg
- 1 teaspoon vanilla essence
- 150 g (5 oz) self-raising flour
- 75 g (3 oz) porridge oats
- 50 g (2 oz) plain or milk chocolate drops
- 50 g (2 oz) white chocolate drops

**1** Help your child to cut out 2 large sheets of baking paper to line the baking sheets while you set the oven to 190°C (375°F), Gas Mark 5.

**2** Place the butter and sugar in the mixing bowl and help your child beat them together either with an electric whisk or a wooden spoon until creamy.

**3** Add the egg and vanilla essence and mix together again. Place the sieve over the mixing bowl, sift in the flour and then mix in.

**4** Add the oats and chocolate drops and stir in, then, using a teaspoon and a finger to scrape the mixture off, place generous spoonfuls of the mixture in 24 or so lumpy heaps on the prepared baking sheets. Allow plenty of space between the heaps as the cookies will spread as they cook.

**5** Bake the cookies for about 10 minutes, until the ones on the top shelf are golden brown, then remove them from the oven and move the other baking sheet up from the bottom shelf. Bake these for a further 3–5 minutes until they are golden, then remove.

**6** Cool the cookies on the baking sheets for a few minutes before transferring, with a fish slice or palette knife, to a cooling rack. The cookies will crisp up as they cool.

**COOKIES WILL CRISP UP**
AS THEY COOL DOWN

# Coconut racoons

**MAKES** about 20  **PREP TIME** 15 minutes  **COOKING TIME** 20 minutes

**Discs of coconut macaroon with one side dipped in melted chocolate to give them a stripy, racoon look. We like these with vanilla ice cream.**

## Equipment

nonstick baking paper • scissors • 2 large baking sheets • large mixing bowl • hand-held electric whisk or hand whisk • large metal spoon • teaspoon • egg cup • fish slice or palette knife • cooling rack • small heatproof bowl • small saucepan • wooden spoon

## Ingredients

- 3 egg whites
- 100 g (3½ oz) golden caster sugar
- 200 g (7 oz) desiccated coconut
- 100 g (3½ oz) plain chocolate, broken into small pieces, to decorate

**1** Ask your child to cut out 2 sheets of the baking paper to line the baking sheets while you set the oven to 160°C (325°F), Gas Mark 3.

**2** Place the egg whites in a mixing bowl and help your child to use an electric or hand whisk to beat the whites until they form peaks when you turn off (if electric) and lift up the whisk.

**3** Add about one-third of the sugar and whisk it in. Add another third and whisk that in, then the final third.

**4** Add the coconut and, using a large metal spoon, show your child how to fold it in gently so as not to knock the air out of the mixture.

**5** Use a teaspoon to fill an egg cup with the mixture and then tip out mounds on to the prepared baking sheets, leaving a little space between each one.

**6** Bake the macaroons for 15 minutes or until the tops are golden brown. Leave to cool on the baking sheets for 2–3 minutes, then remove with a fish slice or palette knife to a cooling rack.

**7** Meanwhile, melt the chocolate by placing it in the heatproof bowl over a small saucepan of simmering water. When the chocolate has melted, stir, remove the bowl from the pan and allow to cool a little.

**8** Help your child to dip the cool macaroons into the chocolate and place on fresh pieces of baking paper until set.

**9** When set, peel the macaroons off the paper with a palette knife or fish slice.

**CUT OUT STARS**
USING A COOKIE CUTTER

# Sparkly starfish

**MAKES** about 100   **PREP TIME** 30 minutes   **COOKING TIME** 10 minutes

**Buttery shortbread cut into tiny stars and decorated with sparkly sugar, these little biscuits make great presents stacked into a cellophane bag and tied with a pretty ribbon.**

## Equipment

nonstick baking paper • scissors • 2 large baking sheets • mixing bowl • small star or other shaped cutter • pastry brush

## Ingredients

- 150 g (5 oz) plain flour, plus extra for dusting
- 3 tablespoons rice flour
- 50 g (2 oz) caster sugar
- 100 g (3½ oz) butter, softened
- few drops of green food colouring
- 1 small egg, beaten
- 25 g (1 oz) demerara sugar or coloured sugar cake decorations

**1** Help your child to cut out 2 large sheets of baking paper to line the baking sheets while you set the oven to 160°C (325°F), Gas Mark 3.

**2** Place the flour, rice flour and sugar in the mixing bowl and have your child mix them together with their hands. Add the butter in one or two big lumps and let your child work it into the dry ingredients with their fingers, squishing and kneading it into a soft dough. (See tips on kneading dough on page 10.)

**3** Add the colouring and squish the dough until the colouring is evenly mixed through and you have a light green dough.

**4** Dust the work surface with flour and place the dough into the middle. Help your child press out and flatten the dough with the ball of their hand until it is about 5 mm (¼ inch) thick.

**5** Show your child how to use a floured cutter to cut out the shapes, then place them on the prepared baking sheets. Keep squishing the leftover bits of pastry together until you can't cut out any more stars.

**6** Brush the shapes with a little egg and then sprinkle with the demerara sugar or cake decorations. Bake for 10 minutes or until golden around the edges.

**7** Remove the biscuits from the oven and leave on the baking sheets until cool. Store in an airtight container.

**TINY TIP** Rice flour gives the biscuits a slightly crunchy texture but can be omitted, in which case use 175 g (6 oz) plain flour.

# Down-under biccies

**MAKES** 16   **PREP TIME** 15 minutes   **COOKING TIME** 20 minutes

**This recipe is based on the Australian and New Zealand Anzac biscuits made to commemorate soldiers who gave their lives in both world wars.**

## Equipment

2 large baking sheets • large saucepan • small bowl or ramekin • teaspoon • wooden spoon • large mixing bowl • fish slice • cooling rack

## Ingredients

- cooking oil, for greasing
- 150 g (5 oz) butter
- 1 tablespoon golden syrup
- 1 tablespoon boiling water
- 1 teaspoon bicarbonate of soda
- 100 g (3½ oz) porridge oats
- 100 g (3½ oz) plain flour
- 50 g (2 oz) desiccated coconut
- 100 g (3½ oz) soft light brown sugar

**1** Sprinkle a few drops of cooking oil on each of the baking sheets and have your little one smear it all over with their fingers. Set the oven to 160°C (325°F), Gas Mark 3.

**2** Place the butter and syrup in the saucepan and heat gently. Place the boiling water in a small bowl or ramekin and have your child add the bicarbonate of soda and stir it in with a teaspoon. Add this to the syrup, stir and watch it fizz.

**3** Place all the remaining ingredients in a large bowl and let your child mix them together with their hands, then tip the mixture into the saucepan and stir well to combine.

**4** Show your child how to pile small spoonfuls of the mixture on to the prepared baking sheets using the teaspoon, leaving plenty of space between each pile to allow the biscuits to spread as they cook.

**5** Bake the biscuits for 15 minutes until golden brown, then remove them from the oven and allow to cool for 5 minutes on the baking sheets before transferring to a cooling rack with a fish slice.

# Monkey nut cookies

**MAKES** 20   **PREP TIME** 20 minutes   **COOKING TIME** 12–15 minutes

### These are proper cookies with a slightly dense, fudgy centre and a crispy outside.

## Equipment

nonstick baking paper • scissors • 2 large baking sheets • large mixing bowl • wooden spoon or hand-held electric whisk • sieve • teaspoon • fish slice or palette knife • cooling rack

## Ingredients

- 100 g (3½ oz) butter or margarine, softened
- 100 g (3½ oz) smooth peanut butter
- 150 g (5 oz) soft light brown sugar
- 1 egg
- 200 g (7 oz) plain flour
- ¼ teaspoon baking powder
- ¼ teaspoon bicarbonate of soda

**1** Show your child how to cut out 2 large sheets of the baking paper to fit the baking sheets while you set the oven to 190ºC (375ºF), Gas Mark 5.

**2** Place the butter, peanut butter and sugar in a bowl and help your child beat them together with a wooden spoon or hand-held electric whisk until smooth.

**3** Crack the egg and have your child carefully break it into the mix. Stir together.

**4** Balance the sieve on top of the bowl, add the flour, baking powder and bicarbonate of soda, sift in and mix well.

**5** Help your child put heaped teaspoonfuls of the mixture on to the prepared baking sheets, leaving plenty of space between each pile.

**6** Bake the cookies for 12–15 minutes or until they are light golden with firm edges but still have slightly soft centres. Remove them from the oven and, with a fish slice or palette knife, transfer immediately to a cooling rack.

**SMOOTH PEANUT BUTTER**
IS BEST FOR THIS RECIPE

# Gingerbread royalty

**MAKES** 12 **PREP TIME** 30 minutes, plus chilling **COOKING TIME** 10–15 minutes

## Let your little one's imagination run riot decorating these figures.

## Equipment

nonstick baking paper • scissors • 2 large baking sheets • large mixing bowl • wooden spoon or hand-held electric whisk • sieve • clingfilm • rolling pin • gingerbread men and women cutters • palette knife • cooling rack

## Ingredients

- 100 g (3½ oz) butter or margarine, softened
- 100 g (3½ oz) caster sugar
- 1 egg
- few drops of vanilla essence
- 200 g (7 oz) self-raising flour, plus extra for dusting
- 1 tablespoon ground ginger
- small sweets, to decorate
- icing pens, to decorate
- cake decorations, to decorate

**1** Help your child to cut 2 large sheets of baking paper to cover the baking sheets.

**2** Place the butter and sugar in a large mixing bowl and beat until creamy.

**3** Crack the egg for your child and let them break it carefully into the mixture. Add the vanilla essence and mix again until smooth.

**4** Sift the flour and ginger into the mixing bowl, then stir with a wooden spoon to make a soft dough. Have your child put their hands in the bowl and pull all the bits together into a ball. If the dough is very sticky, add a little more flour.

**5** Wrap the dough in clingfilm and chill in the refrigerator for 1 hour. When chilled, dust a work surface with flour and help your little one roll or press out the dough with their fingers until it is about 5 mm (¼ inch) thick.

**6** Preheat the oven to 180°C (350°F), Gas Mark 4. Show your child how to use the cutters and place the shapes on the prepared baking sheets using a palette knife.

**7** Bake the biscuits for 10–15 minutes or until a pale golden colour. Transfer to a cooling rack and leave to cool.

**8** When the gingerbread figures have cooled down, decorate them using sweetie jewels, icing pens and cake decorations.

# Jammy dodgers

**MAKES** 20  **PREP TIME** 30 minutes, plus chilling  **COOKING TIME** 10–15 minutes

## Much better than the shop-bought variety, with lots of gooey jam.

## Equipment

nonstick baking paper • scissors
• 2 large baking sheets • large
mixing bowl • wooden spoon or
hand-held electric whisk • sieve
• clingfilm • rolling pin • round
cutters • plastic drinking straws
• cooling rack • teaspoon

## Ingredients

• 100 g (3½ oz) butter or margarine,
  softened
• 100 g (3½ oz) caster sugar
• 1 egg
• few drops of vanilla essence
• 225 g (7½ oz) plain flour, plus extra
  for dusting
FOR THE FILLING
• 3–4 tablespoons raspberry or
  strawberry jam

**1** Help your child to cut 2 large sheets of baking paper to cover the baking sheets.

**2** Place the butter and sugar in a large mixing bowl and beat together until creamy.

**3** Crack the egg for your child and let them break it carefully into the mixture. Add the vanilla essence and mix again until smooth.

**4** Sift in the flour and stir to make a soft dough. Have your child put their hands in the bowl and pull all the bits into a ball. If the dough is very sticky, add a little more flour.

**5** Wrap the dough in clingfilm and chill for 1 hour. Set the oven to 180°C (350°F), Gas Mark 4. Dust a work surface with flour and help your little one roll or press out the dough with their fingers until it is about 5 mm (¼ inch) thick.

**6** Show your child how to use the cutters. Cut 2 circles for each dodger, then use a straw to cut out the eyes and mouth on half the circles. Place the shapes on the prepared baking sheets.

**7** Bake the biscuits for 10–15 minutes or until a pale golden colour. Transfer to a cooling rack and leave to cool.

**8** Take a pair of biscuits and spread ½ teaspoon of jam on the bottom one. Place the other circle with the face on top and sandwich together. Repeat with the remaining biscuits.

# Vanilla flowers

**MAKES** 30  **PREP TIME** 30 minutes  **COOKING TIME** 10–15 minutes

Here's a chance for your child to try their hand at piping. Mastering the piping bag can be tricky but the process is very exciting.

## Equipment

nonstick baking paper • scissors • 2 large baking sheets • large mixing bowl • sieve • wooden spoon • large metal spoon • piping bag fitted with a 1 cm (½ inch) star nozzle • knife • cooling rack • fish slice or palette knife

## Ingredients

- 200 g (7 oz) butter, softened
- few drops of vanilla essence
- 50 g (2 oz) icing sugar
- 175 g (6 oz) plain flour
- 50 g (2 oz) cornflour
- cake decorations, to decorate

**1** Show your child how to cut 2 sheets of baking paper to fit the baking sheets. Place the butter and vanilla essence in the mixing bowl and help your child to sift in the icing sugar, then cream the ingredients together with the wooden spoon.

**2** Sift in the flour and the cornflour a little at a time and fold in with the metal spoon. Fold back the piping bag so that the top is halfway down the bag. Spoon in the mixture and then fold the bag back up and twist it together from the top down to the mixture.

**3** Show your child how to hold on or near the nozzle with one hand and the twisted bag with the other. As they squeeze the bag, the mixture should be forced out. Continue to twist the bag down as mixture is piped out.

**4** Pipe the mixture on to the prepared baking sheets in little flower shapes. To finish a flower, push the nozzle down into the piped flower as you stop squeezing. If your child cannot manage this, help them by cutting the mixture with a knife to finish each flower.

**5** While your child is piping, set the oven to 190°C (375°F), Gas Mark 5.

**6** When all the flowers are piped, your child can press a decoration into the centre of each one.

**7** Bake the cookies for 10–15 minutes or until they are a pale golden colour. Remove from the oven and allow to cool for a few minutes on the baking sheets before transferring to a cooling rack with a fish slice or palette knife.

# Frangipane wheels

**MAKES** 15   **PREP TIME** 15 minutes   **COOKING TIME** 15 minutes

These light and crispy pastries are very quick to make. They are great as a dessert too, served with stewed fruit, fruit fool or yogurt.

## Equipment

nonstick baking paper • scissors • 2 large baking sheets • rolling pin • tablespoon • dessertspoon • sharp knife

## Ingredients

- 375 g (12 oz) ready-rolled puff pastry, thawed if frozen and taken out of the refrigerator 15 minutes before use
- 250 g (8 oz) white marzipan
- 2 tablespoons raspberry or strawberry jam
- plain flour, icing sugar and caster sugar, for dusting

**1** Have your child dust the work surface with a little plain flour while you set the oven to 180°C (350°F), Gas Mark 4. Help them to cut a piece of baking paper to line each baking sheet.

**2** Unroll the pastry on to the flour-dusted work surface and pat it down gently with your fingertips. Alongside, dust the work surface with icing sugar and help your child roll the marzipan out to the same size as the pastry rectangle.

**3** Place the marzipan on top of the pastry. Dollop the jam into the middle of the marzipan and spread it thinly all over with a dessertspoon.

**4** Roll up the pastry and marzipan together to make a long sausage shape.

**5** Using a sharp knife, cut the roll into 1 cm (½ inch) slices. Help your child place each slice on the prepared baking sheets.

**6** Bake the pastries for 15 minutes or until puffed and golden. Transfer to a cooling rack.

**7** Let your child sprinkle the pastries with caster sugar while still warm.

# Smarty pants

**MAKES** 20    **PREP TIME** 20 minutes, plus chilling    **COOKING TIME** 10–15 minutes

### Make a template for these cute biscuits by drawing a simple trouser shape on thin card, then help your child to cut around the shape.

## Equipment

nonstick baking paper • scissors
• 2 large baking sheets • large
mixing bowl • wooden spoon or
hand-held electric whisk • sieve
• clingfilm • rolling pin • trouser-
shaped template and sharp knife
(or cutter) • cooling rack

## Ingredients

• 100 g (3½ oz) butter or margarine,
  softened
• 100 g (3½ oz) caster sugar
• 1 egg
• few drops of vanilla essence
• 200 g (7 oz) self-raising flour,
  plus extra for dusting
• 3 tablespoons cocoa powder
• packet of sweets, to decorate

**1** Help your child to cut 2 large sheets of baking paper to cover the baking sheets while you set the oven to 180°C (350°F), Gas Mark 4.

**2** Help your child to place the butter and sugar in a large mixing bowl and beat together until creamy.

**3** Crack the egg for your child and let them break it carefully into the mixture. Add the vanilla essence and mix again until smooth.

**4** Sift in the flour and cocoa powder, then stir to make a soft dough. Have your child put their hands in the bowl and pull all the bits together into a ball. If the dough is very sticky add a little more flour.

**5** Wrap the dough in clingfilm and chill in the refrigerator for 1 hour.

**6** Dust a work surface with flour and help your little one roll or press out the dough with their fingers until it is about 5 mm (¼ inch) thick.

**7** Help them cut around the template and place the trouser shapes on the prepared baking sheets.

**8** Show your child how to press a few sweets into each biscuit.

**9** Bake the biscuits for 10–15 minutes or until a pale golden colour. Transfer to a cooling rack and leave to cool.

CAREFULLY CUT OUT
THE TROUSER TEMPLATE

# Butterfly biscuits

**MAKES** 20    **PREP TIME** 30 minutes, plus chilling    **COOKING TIME** 10–15 minutes

## Here's a chance for your child's creative imagination to run riot.

## Equipment

sieve • large mixing bowl • wooden spoon • measuring jug or small bowl • fork • clingfilm • nonstick baking paper • scissors • 2 large baking sheets • rolling pin • butterfly-shaped cutter • cooling rack • small bowl • hand-held electric whisk (optional) • teaspoon

## Ingredients

- 275 g (9 oz) self-raising flour, plus extra for dusting
- 1 dessertspoon ground cinnamon (optional)
- 100 g (3½ oz) soft light brown sugar
- 75 g (3 oz) butter, cut into pieces
- 1 egg
- 2 tablespoons golden syrup

FOR THE ICING
- 50 g (2 oz) butter, softened
- 150 g (5 oz) icing sugar
- 2 teaspoons milk
- few drops of food colouring (optional)
- cake decorations or small sweets, to decorate
- icing pens, to decorate

**1** Sift the flour and cinnamon, if using, into a large mixing bowl. Stir in the sugar.

**2** Add the butter pieces. Show your child how to rub the mixture together with their fingertips until it resembles breadcrumbs.

**3** Crack the egg and have your child carefully break it into the measuring jug. Add the syrup and let them beat it with a fork. Add to the flour mix and stir into a ball. Wrap the dough in clingfilm and chill for 1 hour.

**4** Meanwhile, set the oven to 170°C (340°F), Gas Mark 3½. Help your child to cut 2 large sheets of the baking paper to line the baking sheets.

**5** Sprinkle some flour on the work surface and place the chilled dough in the middle. Help your child to roll or press out the dough to a thickness of 5 mm (¼ inch).

**6** Show your child how to use a butterfly-shaped cutter to cut out about 20 biscuits.

**7** Bake the biscuits for 10–15 minutes or until golden brown around the edges, then remove from the oven. Allow to cool on the baking sheets for a few minutes, then transfer to the cooling rack to cool completely.

**8** Meanwhile, make the butter icing by mixing the ingredients together in a small bowl with a wooden spoon or hand-held electric whisk.

**9** Use a teaspoon to spread the icing over the cool biscuits. Decorate by pressing in small sweets and/or cake decorations and drawing with the icing pens.

**CUT OUT BUTTERFLIES**
USING A COOKIE CUTTER

**BEAT THE MIXTURE**
WITH A WOODEN SPOON

# Soft blueberry cookies

**MAKES** 12    **PREP TIME** 15 minutes    **COOKING TIME** 12–15 minutes

**These cookies are soft, scrumptious and
full of those oh-so-good-for-you-and-still-utterly
delicious blueberries.**

## Equipment

nonstick baking paper • scissors
• 2 large baking sheets • large
mixing bowl • hand-held electric
whisk or wooden spoon • sieve •
dessertspoon • cooling rack • fish
slice or palette knife

## Ingredients

- 75 g (3 oz) butter or margarine,
  softened
- 125 g (4 oz) soft light brown sugar
- 1 egg
- 1 teaspoon vanilla essence
- 175 g (6 oz) self-raising flour
- grated rind of an unwaxed lemon
- 125 g (4 oz) blueberries

**1** Show your little one how to cut out 2 large sheets of
the baking paper to line the baking sheets while you
set the oven to 180°C (350°F), Gas Mark 4.

**2** Place the butter and sugar in the mixing bowl and
help your child beat them together until creamy either
with a hand-held electric whisk or a wooden spoon.

**3** Add the egg and vanilla essence and beat again, then
place the sieve over the mixing bowl and sift in the
flour. Finally, add the lemon rind and mix together.

**4** Show your child how to place dessertspoonfuls of the
mixture on the prepared baking sheets, then use the
back of the spoon to spread the mounds into rounds.
Leave plenty of space between the rounds to allow
the biscuits to spread when cooking. Place 5 or 6
blueberries on top of each cookie.

**5** Bake the cookies for 12–15 minutes until a pale
golden colour, then remove from the oven and allow
to cool for a few minutes before transferring to a
cooling rack with a fish slice or palette knife to cool
and crisp up.

# Easy Peasy

# Chocolate scribble cake

**MAKES** 9 squares   **PREP TIME** 20 minutes   **COOKING TIME** 25 minutes

### A really quick and easy chocolate brownie-style sponge mixture, which is decorated with glacé icing scribbles.

## Equipment

shallow cake tin, 20 cm (8 inches) square • nonstick baking paper • pencil • scissors • small heatproof bowl • small saucepan • large mixing bowl • sieve • wooden spoon or whisk • spatula • knife

## Ingredients

- 50 g (2 oz) butter or margarine
- 50 g (2 oz) plain chocolate, broken into small pieces
- 2 eggs
- 150 g (5 oz) soft light brown sugar
- 50 g (2 oz) self-raising flour
- icing pens, to decorate

**1** Set the oven to 180°C (350°F), Gas Mark 4. Place the tin on a piece of baking paper and show your child how to draw around it with the pencil and then cut it out. Place the paper in the bottom of the baking tin.

**2** Place the butter and chocolate in a small heatproof bowl. Boil the kettle and pour approximately 5 cm (2 inches) of water into the small pan and then place on a low heat.

**3** Place the heatproof bowl containing the chocolate and butter over this simmering water so that it is suspended on the top of the saucepan and the chocolate will melt slowly.

**4** Break the eggs into a large mixing bowl, then add the sugar and sift in the flour. Ask your child to stir them together vigorously.

**5** Stir the melted chocolate and butter and carefully pour it into the mixing bowl. Ask your child to stir the mixture until you have a smooth chocolate goo.

**6** Pour the mixture into the tin using the spatula to scrape every last bit from the bowl, then place on the top shelf of the preheated oven for 20 minutes or until just firm when you touch it very gently in the middle of the top.

**7** Allow the cake to cool in the tin and then cut it into 9 pieces in the tin.

**8** Ask your child to decorate the squares with icing pens, perhaps drawing pictures of each family member on that person's piece of cake.

STIR THE CHOCOLATE
INTO THE MIXTURE

# Queen of hearts' tarts

**MAKES** 12   **PREP TIME** 30 minutes   **COOKING TIME** 15 minutes

### These very simple jammy tarts will introduce your child to the pleasures of cutting and eating pastry.

## Equipment

kitchen paper • 12-cup bun tray •
8 cm (3¼ inch) plain or fluted round
cutter • rolling pin • fork • cooking
foil or baking paper • baking beans •
teaspoon • small palette knife •
cooling rack

## Ingredients

- knob of softened butter or
  margarine, for greasing
- plain flour, for dusting
- 375 g (12 oz) ready-rolled
  shortcrust pastry, thawed if frozen
- approx 100 g (3½ oz) jam
  (or selection, such as apricot,
  strawberry, blackcurrant,
  lemon curd)

**1** Set the oven to 220°C (425°F), Gas Mark 7. Using a sheet of kitchen paper, ask your little one to help you smear the butter around each of the cups in the bun tray so the pastry will not stick.

**2** Dust a work surface with flour and unroll the pastry sheet so that it lies flat. Show your child how to cut circles in the pastry with the pastry cutter. Any leftover pastry can be squished together into a ball, then rolled out again with a rolling pin so further circles can be cut with the pastry cutter. Place each circle in a cup in the bun tray and gently press it down.

**3** Use a fork to pierce the bottom of each circle to let out any air. Tear up small pieces of cooking foil or baking paper (about 5 cm (2 inches) square). Help your child gently press a piece into each pastry case, then fill each one with baking beans.

**4** Place the cases in the oven for 5 minutes, then take out and remove the baking beans and foil. Return to the oven for a further 5 minutes or until the tart cases are golden brown on the edges and just hardened on the bottoms.

**5** Ask your child to help you place teaspoons of jam in each pastry case until they are two-thirds full.

**6** Put the tarts back in the oven for a further 5 minutes. Use a small palette knife to loosen and remove each tart from its case and place on a cooling rack. Allow to cool completely before eating.

**SMEAR BUTTER AROUND**
THE BUN TRAY CUPS

**DECORATE EACH MUFFIN** WITH A BLUEBERRY ON TOP

# Iced blueberry muffins

**MAKES** 12   **PREP TIME** 20 minutes   **COOKING TIME** 20 minutes

### If you enjoy blueberries and white chocolate as much as we do, you'll love these muffins.

## Equipment

12 paper muffin cases • 12-cup muffin tin • large mixing bowl • 2 wooden spoons • sieve • dessertspoon • small saucepan • tablespoon • sieve or strainer • small mixing bowl • large serving plate • teaspoon

## Ingredients

- 150 g (5 oz) caster sugar
- 50 g (2 oz) butter or margarine, softened
- 1 egg
- 150 g (5 oz) self-raising flour
- 100 ml (3½ fl oz) milk
- 1 teaspoon vanilla essence
- 100 g (3½ oz) fresh blueberries
- 50 g (2 oz) white chocolate drops

FOR THE ICING

- 25 g (1 oz) fresh blueberries, plus extra, to decorate
- 4 tablespoons water
- 125 g (4 oz) icing sugar

**1** Set the oven to 190°C (375°F), Gas Mark 5, and ask your child to place the paper cases in the muffin tin.

**2** Place the sugar and butter in a large mixing bowl and ask your child to mash them together vigorously with a wooden spoon. Help your child to add the egg by cracking it for them first.

**3** Ask your child to sift in the flour and stir it in too, but only briefly. Finally, have them add the milk, vanilla essence, blueberries and white chocolate drops and quickly stir them in too. Using a dessertspoon, get you child to fill the paper muffin cases two-thirds full.

**4** Bake for 15 minutes, then leave the cooked muffins to cool in the tin.

**5** Make the icing by placing a handful of the fresh blueberries in a small saucepan with the water and heat gently on the hob. Mash the blueberries with the back of a wooden spoon until you have a bright purple mush, then remove from the heat and strain through a sieve or strainer into a small mixing bowl.

**6** Sift in the icing sugar and stir together to make a smooth, purple glacé icing.

**7** Place the muffins on a large serving plate and ask your child to drizzle the icing on to the tops of the muffins with a teaspoon. Decorate the iced muffins by pressing a nice fat blueberry on to the top of each one.

**STIR THE SYRUP INTO** THE PUFFED RICE MIXTURE

# Crispy crowns

**MAKES** 20  **PREP TIME** 15 minutes  **COOKING TIME** 5 minutes

**These crispy cakes inset with dried fruit and fruit flake jewels are perfect for parties.**

## Equipment

scissors • medium mixing bowl • wooden spoon • small paper cake cases • large serving plate or tray • small saucepan • dessertspoon • teaspoon

## Ingredients

- 25 g (1 oz) dried apricots
- 50 g (2 oz) puffed rice
- 20 g (¾ oz) pack strawberry fruit flakes or dried cranberries
- 20 g (¾ oz) pack blackcurrant fruit flakes or dried blueberries
- 1 tablespoon golden syrup or runny honey
- 50 g (2 oz) caster sugar
- 50 g (2 oz) butter or margarine

**1** Use a clean pair of scissors to cut the dried apricots into small pieces in a mixing bowl. It will depend on the age of your child as to whether they will be able to manage this. Add the puffed rice and fruit flakes and stir them together.

**2** Ask your child to set out 20 or so small paper cases on a large serving plate or tray.

**3** Place the syrup or honey, sugar and butter in a small saucepan and heat gently until just bubbling. Stir together, then remove from the heat and allow to cool for 5 minutes.

**4** Help your child to pour the cooled syrup over the puffed rice mixture and stir it all together with a dessertspoon until the rice is covered in the sticky syrup mix.

**5** Show your child how to take a heaped teaspoon of the mixture to fill each case, but work quickly as the mixture will set as it cools.

# Dotty brownies

**MAKES** 16   **PREP TIME** 20 minutes   **COOKING TIME** 25 minutes

## These fantastically gooey, chewy brownies are dotted with white chocolate.

## Equipment

cake tin, 20 cm (8 inches) square • nonstick baking paper • pencil • scissors • small heatproof mixing bowl • small saucepan • large mixing bowl • wooden spoon • sieve • spatula • knife

## Ingredients

- 150 g (5 oz) plain chocolate, broken into small pieces
- 125 ml (4 fl oz) sunflower, vegetable or peanut oil
- 200 g (7 oz) soft light brown sugar
- 2 eggs
- 75 g (3 oz) self-raising flour
- 4 tablespoons cocoa powder
- 50 g (2 oz) white chocolate drops or buttons

**TINY TIP** If you wish, add pieces of walnuts or pecan nuts to the mixture.

**1** Set the oven to 180°C (350°F), Gas Mark 4. Place the cake tin on a piece of baking paper and get your child to draw around it with a pencil. Cut out the square and use it to line the cake tin.

**2** Place the chocolate in the small heatproof bowl. Boil a kettle and pour approximately 5 cm (2 in) of water into the small pan and then place on a low heat.

**3** Place the bowl containing the chocolate over this simmering water so that it is suspended on the top of the saucepan and the chocolate will melt slowly.

**4** Place the oil, sugar and eggs in the large mixing bowl and ask your child to stir them vigorously with the wooden spoon.

**5** When melted, pour the chocolate into the mixture and stir it in.

**6** Sift the flour and cocoa powder into the mixture. Mix this in and then pour the mixture into the prepared tin. Help your child to use the spatula to scrape out the bowl so every last bit is used.

**7** Ask your child to scatter handfuls of the white chocolate drops over the top of the mixture in the tin.

**8** Place the tin on the top shelf of the oven and bake for 20 minutes. The brownies should still be slightly soft in the centre. Leave in the tin to cool, then cut into 16 pieces.

# Scrummy soft flapjacks

**MAKES** 12   **PREP TIME** 15 minutes   **COOKING TIME** 25–30 minutes

## A soft, buttery oat flapjack made with a splash of apple juice and decorated with chocolate drops.

### Equipment

nonstick baking paper • pencil • scissors • cake tin, 20 cm (8 inches) square • large saucepan • wooden spoon • sharp knife • palette knife • serving plate

### Ingredients

- 150 g (5 oz) butter
- 75 g (3 oz) soft light brown sugar
- 75 g (3 oz) golden syrup
- 50 ml (2 fl oz) apple juice
- 225 g (7½ oz) porridge oats
- 50 g (2 oz) white or milk chocolate drops

**1** Set the oven to 180°C (350°F), Gas Mark 4. Take a piece of baking paper and lay it on the work surface, then have your child place the cake tin on top and draw around it with a pencil. Cut out the square of baking paper and use it to line the tin.

**2** Help your child measure out the butter, sugar and golden syrup into a large saucepan and then place it on a gentle heat on the hob for them. Stir until the mixture has melted and is just starting to bubble.

**3** Remove the pan from the heat and add the apple juice and the oats, then stir together until all the oats are evenly covered. Tip the mixture into the prepared tin and help your child to use the wooden spoon to spread the mixture into all the corners and smooth the surface.

**4** Ask your child to sprinkle handfuls of the chocolate drops over the flapjacks.

**5** Bake the flapjacks for 20–25 minutes or until they are a deep golden colour. Be aware that they will still look very soft when they are hot but will set as they cool. Remove from the oven and slice into about 12 even-sized pieces but leave in the tin to cool completely.

**6** When the flapjacks are cool, ask your child to remove them from the tin with the palette knife and then place them on a serving plate.

# Crescent moon cookies

**MAKES** 16   **PREP TIME** 30 minutes   **COOKING TIME** 20–25 minutes

### Little almond-flavoured soft cookies that are fun to shape.

## Equipment

nonstick baking paper • scissors • baking sheet • large mixing bowl • wooden spoon or hand-held electric whisk • sieve • fish slice • cooling rack

## Ingredients

- 50 g (2 oz) caster sugar
- 100 g (3½ oz) butter or margarine, softened
- 1 tablespoon water
- 1 teaspoon almond essence
- 150 g (5 oz) plain flour, plus extra for dusting hands
- 75 g (3 oz) ground almonds
- icing sugar, for dusting

**1** Show your child how to cut a large sheet of the baking paper to fit the baking sheet while you set the oven to 160°C (325°F), Gas Mark 3.

**2** Place the sugar and butter in the mixing bowl and get your child to mash them together vigorously with a wooden spoon, or a hand-held electric whisk if they can manage one, until they are thoroughly mixed and creamy.

**3** Add the water and almond essence and stir in. Finally, sift in the flour and add the ground almonds, then gently stir the mixture together until you have a soft dough.

**4** Dip your and your little one's hands in flour to stop the dough sticking. Pick up walnut-sized pieces of the dough and shape into crescents by rolling into sausages with fatter middles and curved ends. Place on the prepared baking sheet.

**5** Bake the biscuits for 20–25 minutes or until they are set and golden. Remove from the oven and allow to cool on the baking sheet for 10 minutes, then transfer with a fish slice to a cooling rack.

**6** When the cookies are completely cool, dust them with icing sugar.

**DUST WITH ICING SUGAR**
WHEN THE COOKIES ARE COOL

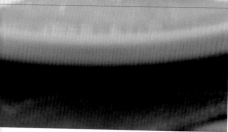

**ROLL THE MIXTURE**
INTO SMALL BALLS

# Marzipan buttons

**MAKES** 30  **PREP TIME** 45 minutes  **COOKING TIME** 7 minutes

## Little cookies sandwiched with a soft marzipan centre and drizzled with chocolate.

### Equipment

nonstick baking paper • scissors • 2 baking sheets • large mixing bowl • hand-held electric whisk or hand whisk • sieve • wooden spoon • knife • small saucepan • small heatproof bowl • cooling rack • teaspoon

### Ingredients

- 200 g (7 oz) butter, softened
- 200 g (7 oz) soft light brown sugar
- 1 egg, beaten
- 1 teaspoon vanilla essence
- 300 g (10 oz) plain flour, plus extra for dusting hands
- 200 g (7 oz) marzipan paste
- 100 g (3½ oz) milk or white chocolate

**1** Ask your child to cut 2 large sheets of the baking paper to fit the baking sheets while you set the oven to 170°C (340°F), Gas Mark 3½.

**2** Place the butter and sugar in the mixing bowl. Help your child mix with an electric or hand whisk until the mixture is pale and fluffy. Add the egg and vanilla essence, then beat again. Sift in the flour and stir with a wooden spoon.

**3** Dip your little one's hand in flour to stop the mixture sticking. Show your child how to take walnut-sized pieces of the mixture, roll them into balls, then place on the baking sheets and flatten slightly into circles.

**4** When there are about 30 dough circles (which should use just over half the mixture), cut the marzipan into 30 even-sized pieces and have your child roll these into balls, then put one in the middle of each cookie.

**5** Take slightly smaller amounts of the remaining dough mixture and gently flatten on top of the marzipan to sandwich it and gently press the edges together. Put the baking sheets in the oven and bake for 7 minutes.

**6** Meanwhile, boil some water in the saucepan and set the heatproof bowl on top. Break the chocolate into the bowl and allow to melt slowly, then stir until smooth.

**7** Remove the cookies from the oven and allow to cool on the baking sheets for a few minutes before transferring to a cooling rack.

**8** Use a teaspoon to drizzle the melted chocolate over the cookies to decorate. Cool before serving.

# Funny faces

**MAKES** 12   **PREP TIME** 20 minutes   **COOKING TIME** 20 minutes

A very simple cake mix, like Butterfly cakes
(see page 80), but decorated to make funny faces.
They were a big hit at my daughter's school fair
and caused an excited rush to the cake stall.

## Equipment

12 paper cake cases • 12-cup bun
tray • large mixing bowl • wooden
spoon or hand-held electric whisk •
sieve • dessertspoon • cooling rack •
2 medium mixing bowls • teaspoon

## Ingredients

- 100 g (3½ oz) butter or margarine,
  softened
- 100 g (3½ oz) caster sugar
- 2 eggs
- 100 g (3½ oz) self-raising flour
- 3 tablespoons cocoa powder

FOR THE ICING

- 75 g (3 oz) butter, softened
- 175 g (6 oz) icing sugar, sifted
- 1 tablespoon milk or water
- 2–3 drops of red food colouring
  and/or 2 tablespoons cocoa powder

TO DECORATE

- icing pens
- white and milk chocolate buttons
- cake decorations

**1** Show your child how to place a paper case in each
of the cups in the bun tray while you set the oven
to 180°C (350°F), Gas Mark 4.

**2** Place the butter and sugar in the mixing bowl and
beat together with the wooden spoon or electric
whisk until smooth and creamy.

**3** Crack the eggs for your child and then have them
break them into the mixture one at a time, being
careful not to let any shell fall in. Beat the mixture
again between egg additions.

**4** Place the sieve over the mixing bowl and sift in the
flour and cocoa powder, then stir in. Have your child
drop dessertspoonfuls of the mixture into the
prepared cases.

**5** Bake for 20 minutes or until springy to the touch.

**6** Remove from the oven and allow to cool in the tin for
a few minutes, then transfer to a cooling rack and
allow to cool completely.

**7** Meanwhile, prepare the icing. Place the butter, sugar
and milk in a mixing bowl and beat together, then
divide into 2 bowls. Add the colouring to one and the
cocoa powder to the other. Mix in, then leave them in
a cool place.

**8** When the cakes are cool, smooth on the butter icing
with the back of a teaspoon, then use your imagination
to decorate them with lots of different funny faces.

**BREAK THE CHOCOLATE**
INTO A HEATPROOF BOWL

# Rocky road bars

**MAKES** 36   **PREP TIME** 15 minutes, plus chilling   **COOKING TIME** 5 minutes

**These bars could be made by substituting the marshmallows with nuts (such as pistachios, walnuts or pecans).**

## Equipment

small saucepan • small heatproof bowl • 1 kg (2 lb) loaf tin • nonstick baking paper • scissors • wooden spoon • clingfilm • chopping board • sharp knife

## Ingredients

- 100 g (3½ oz) plain chocolate
- 100 g (3½ oz) white chocolate
- 50 g (2 oz) butter
- 100 ml (3½ fl oz) water
- 100 g (3½ oz) digestive or rich tea biscuits, broken into small pieces
- 50 g (2 oz) mini marshmallows
- 50 g (2 oz) golden marzipan, chopped into small pieces

**1** Pour boiling water from the kettle into the small saucepan so that there is about 5 cm (2 inches) in the bottom and set on a low heat.

**2** With help from your child, break the chocolate into small pieces and place in the heatproof bowl. Add the butter and water and set this over the simmering water in the pan.

**3** While the chocolate melts, help your little one to line the loaf tin by cutting out a piece of baking paper to fit.

**4** When the chocolate has melted, let the bowl cool slightly, then have your child carefully stir together the sticky goo.

**5** Add all the other ingredients and stir again until evenly mixed and coated in chocolate. Tip into the prepared tin, push into the corners using the wooden spoon and smooth the top.

**6** Cover the tin with clingfilm and leave to cool completely before putting in the refrigerator for at least 1 hour until it is set.

**7** Turn out the loaf on to a chopping board and use a sharp knife and all your strength to cut into bite-sized pieces or mini bars.

# Butterfly cakes

**MAKES** 12   **PREP TIME** 20 minutes   **COOKING TIME** 20 minutes

Butterfly cakes, or fairy flips as my daughter calls them, are traditional children's party fare. An easy, one-bowl mix your kids will love to make.

## Equipment

12 paper cake cases • 12-cup bun tray • large mixing bowl • wooden spoon or hand-held electric whisk • sieve • dessertspoon • cooling rack • medium mixing bowl • teaspoon • knife

## Ingredients

- 100 g (3½ oz) butter or margarine, softened
- 100 g (3½ oz) caster sugar
- 2 drops of vanilla essence
- 2 eggs
- 100 g (3½ oz) self-raising flour
FOR THE ICING
- 50 g (2 oz) butter, softened
- 125 g (4 oz) icing sugar, sifted
- 2–3 drops of food colouring (optional)
- 1 tablespoon milk or water
- icing sugar, for dusting
- icing pens, to decorate (optional)

1 Show your child how to place a paper case in each of the cups in the bun tray while you set the oven to 180°C (350°F), Gas Mark 4.

2 Place the butter, sugar and vanilla essence in the large mixing bowl and beat together with the wooden spoon or electric whisk until smooth and creamy.

3 Crack the eggs for your child and let them break them into the mixture one at a time, being careful not to let any shell fall in. Beat the mixture again between egg additions.

4 Place the sieve over the mixing bowl, sift in the flour, then stir in. Have your child drop dessertspoonfuls of the mixture into the prepared cases.

5 Bake for 20 minutes or until golden and springy to the touch.

6 Remove from the oven and allow to cool in the tin for a few minutes before transferring to a cooling rack and allowing to cool completely.

7 Meanwhile, make the butter icing. Put the ingredients in a bowl and beat together, then leave in a cool place while the cakes are cooling.

8 Using a teaspoon, dig out a circle 2.5 cm (1 inch) or so in diameter from the top of each cake. Slice the cone-like piece of cake you have dug out in half.

9 Help your child fill the holes in the cakes with the icing, then gently stick the cone halves into the icing so that they stick up like a butterfly perched on top. Dust with icing sugar and/or decorate with icing pens.

# Choc meringue shells

**MAKES** 12   **PREP TIME** 30 minutes   **COOKING TIME** 1½ hours

## Sandwiched together with whipped chantilly cream, these are a crunchy and creamy treat.

## Equipment

nonstick baking paper • scissors •
2 large baking sheets • large
scrupulously clean mixing bowl •
hand-held electric whisk, also very
clean and dry • sieve • large metal
spoon • dessertspoon • cooling rack •
medium mixing bowl • serving plate

## Ingredients

- 4 egg whites
- 175 g (6 oz) caster sugar
- 3 tablespoons cocoa powder

FOR THE FILLING

- 250 ml (8 fl oz) double cream
- 2 drops of vanilla essence
- 1 tablespoon icing sugar, sieved

**1** Ask your child to cut out a large sheet of baking paper to fit each baking sheet while you set the oven to 150°C (300°F), Gas Mark 2.

**2** Place the egg whites in the large mixing bowl and help your child to whisk these until they are stiff enough that your child can hold the bowl upside down and none will fall out!

**3** Add the sugar in three lots, whisking in between each addition. Then sift in the cocoa and fold in with the large metal spoon.

**4** Show your child how to use the dessertspoon and a clean finger to spoon about 12 shell shapes on to each prepared baking sheet.

**5** Bake for 1½ hours until crisp, then allow the meringues to cool completely on a cooling rack.

**6** Meanwhile, make the chantilly cream by whipping the cream with the vanilla essence and icing sugar until stiff enough to form peaks that stay when you lift out the whisk.

**7** Sandwich the meringue shells together with dessertspoonfuls of the cream and place in a pile on the serving plate.

**TINY TIP** Make sure that the bowl and whisk are as scrupulously clean and dry as possible. Even the tiniest speck of oil or water will prevent the egg whites from whisking up to make a stiff and fluffy meringue.

# Something Savoury

# Pizza faces

**MAKES** 2   **PREP TIME** 15 minutes   **COOKING TIME** 15–20 minutes

It's a strange fact but children will eat almost anything that's been made into a face. I've even seen olives pass my daughter's lips, although I'm sure she'd deny it!

## Equipment

large baking sheet • sieve • large mixing bowl • wooden spoon • rolling pin

## Ingredients

- cooking oil, for greasing
- 150g (5 oz) self-raising flour, plus extra for dusting
- 40 g (1½ oz) cold butter, cut into small pieces
- pinch of salt
- 3–4 tablespoons milk
- 1 tablespoon olive oil

FOR THE TOPPING
- 4 tablespoons passata
- strips of pepper, olives, cherry tomatoes, sliced mushrooms, basil leaves, ham slices and pineapple pieces, to garnish
- freshly grated mozzarella cheese, for sprinkling, plus slices for eyes if liked

**1** Sprinkle a few drops of cooking oil on the baking sheet and have your child smear it all over. Set the oven to 180°C (350°F), Gas Mark 4.

**2** Sift the flour into a large mixing bowl and add the butter and salt, then show your child how to rub the ingredients together with their fingertips until the butter is broken up and covered with flour and the mixture resembles fine breadcrumbs.

**3** Add the milk and olive oil and mix with a wooden spoon, then put your hands back into the mixture and gently bring it together into a ball of soft dough.

**4** Divide the dough into 2 and make each into a ball. Scatter some flour over the work surface and place one of the balls in the centre.

**5** Using the rolling pin, help your child roll the dough out to a circle about 10 cm (4 inches) across. Then lay the circle on to the prepared baking sheet and roll out the other one.

**6** Spoon 2 tablespoons of the passata on to the centre of each pizza, then spread out to the edges.

**7** Decorate the pizzas with the toppings. Finally, sprinkle grated cheese over the top.

**8** Bake for 15–20 minutes until the edges are golden brown and the cheese melted and golden.

**SPREAD THE PASSATA**
WITH THE BACK OF THE SPOON

# Bread monsters

**MAKES** 8 **PREP TIME** 30 minutes, plus rising **COOKING TIME** 15–20 minutes

**making bread is easy and great fun. for tiny toddlers you can make up the dough and let them play with it to their heart's content.**

## Equipment

large baking sheet • sieve • large mixing bowl • wooden spoon • scissors • tea towel • pastry brush • oven gloves • cooling rack

## Ingredients

• cooking oil, for greasing
• 350 g (11½ oz) strong white flour, plus extra for dusting
• 1 teaspoon salt
• 3 g (½ a sachet) fast-action dried yeast
• 1 tablespoon vegetable oil
• 200 ml (7 fl oz) pre-boiled warm water
• a few currants, cut in half, to decorate
• 1 egg, beaten, to glaze

**1** Sprinkle a few drops of cooking oil on the baking sheet and have your child smear it all over with their fingers.

**2** Sift the flour and salt in the mixing bowl and add the yeast, vegetable oil and water. Mix together with the wooden spoon, then put your hands into the bowl and draw the mixture together into a firm dough.

**3** If the mixture is too dry to come together, add a little more water. If the mixture is too sticky and sticks to your hands, add some more flour.

**4** Sprinkle flour over the work surface and tip the dough on to it. Have your child knead the dough by pushing, folding and turning it. You can be brutal with it: the more work, the better. Knead it for at least 5 minutes. (See tips for kneading dough on page 10.)

**5** Break the dough into 8 equal pieces and knead into balls. Make a pointy snout at one end of each ball and place on the prepared baking sheet. Leave plenty of space between the rolls as they will double in size. Help your child to make the prickles by snipping into the dough with the tips of scissors. Press halves of currants into the dough for eyes.

**6** Cover the rolls with a clean tea towel. Leave in a warm place for 1 hour or until they have doubled in size.

**7** Set the oven to 230°C (450°F), Gas Mark 8. Brush the rolls with the beaten egg and bake for 15–20 minutes. When the rolls are cooked they'll sound hollow when tapped on the bottom (remember to use oven gloves as they will be hot). Transfer to a cooling rack.

**DRAW AROUND A TINY FOOT**
TO MAKE A TEMPLATE

# Cheesy feet

**MAKES** about 9   **PREP TIME** 10–15 minutes   **COOKING TIME** 10 minutes

**Kids will love these really easy savoury biscuits cut into feet shapes and decorated with tiny red pepper or cherry tomato 'toenails'!**

## Equipment

nonstick baking paper • scissors • large baking sheet • foot-shaped pastry cutter or foot template (see Tiny Tip below) and knife • cooling rack

## Ingredients

- plain flour, for dusting
- 375 g (12 oz) ready-rolled puff pastry, thawed if frozen and taken out of the refrigerator 15 minutes before use
- ½ red pepper or a few cherry tomatoes
- 50 g (2 oz) Parmesan cheese, freshly grated

**TINY TIP** To make a foot template, get your little one to stand on a piece of card, draw around the outline of their foot and cut out.

**1** Set the oven to 180°C (350°F), Gas Mark 4. Cut out a square of baking paper to fit a large baking sheet and place on top of the baking sheet.

**2** Sprinkle a little flour on to the work surface and remove the pastry from its wrapping. Unroll the pastry carefully until it is flat, gently pressing it down with your fingers to flatten any creases and mend any cracks.

**3** Show your child how to use a pastry cutter to cut out about 9 feet shapes. Place them spread apart on the prepared baking sheet. Even very young children will be able to help with this. (If you do not have a foot-shaped pastry cutter, see Tiny Tip below for instructions on making a template. Lay the template on the dough and cut around it with a knife.)

**4** Cut tiny pieces of the pepper or tomato using clean kitchen scissors.

**5** Sprinkle the feet with the grated cheese, then add the pepper or tomato pieces – kids will really enjoy pressing them on to the feet as toenails.

**6** Put the feet in the hot oven, making sure children stand well back, for 10–15 minutes or until golden brown and puffed up. Carefully remove them from the oven and then leave to cool on a cooling rack before tucking in!

# Mini quiches

**MAKES** 18    **PREP TIME** 45 minutes    **COOKING TIME** 20 minutes

These little quiches are fun to make and can be filled with your child's favourite foods. They are great for lunch boxes and picnics too.

## Equipment

2 x 12-cup bun trays • 8 cm (3¼ inch) plain or fluted round cutter • measuring jug • fork • small bowl • dessertspoon

## Ingredients

- cooking oil, for greasing
- plain flour, for dusting
- 375 g (12 oz) ready-rolled shortcrust pastry, thawed if frozen and taken out of the refrigerator 15 minutes before use
- 2 eggs
- 200 ml (7 fl oz) milk
- pinch of salt
- 4 slices of ham, diced
- 2 spring onions, chopped
- 5 cherry tomatoes, chopped
- 50 g (2 oz) Cheddar cheese, grated

**1** Set the oven to 220°C (425°F), Gas Mark 7, and sprinkle some oil into the cups of the bun trays. Ask your child to smear the oil all over the cups.

**2** Sprinkle some flour on to a work surface and unroll the pastry. Have your child flatten it with the balls of their hands.

**3** Show them how to stamp circles out of the pastry with the cutter and place each circle in a cup of the tin, gently pressing it down with their fingertips.

**4** Place the eggs, milk and salt in a measuring jug and beat with a fork.

**5** Put the ham, spring onions and cherry tomatoes into a bowl and mix together. Ask your little one to put a dessertspoonful of the mixture into each pastry cup.

**6** Pour some of the egg and milk mixture into each cup.

**7** Sprinkle some grated cheese over the top of each mini quiche.

**8** Bake the quiches for 20 minutes or until set and golden. Eat them hot or cold.

**SPOON THE MIXTURE**
INTO EACH PASTRY CUP

# Money bags

**MAKES** 8   **PREP TIME** 30 minutes   **COOKING TIME** 5–10 minutes

### Filo pastry is great to paint with a pastry brush and these frilly bags are spectacular and tasty.

## Equipment

large baking sheet • 2 small bowls • wooden spoon • tea towel • sharp knife • pastry brush • teaspoon

## Ingredients

- 100 ml (3½ fl oz) cooking oil
- 100 g (3½ oz) feta cheese, chopped into small dice
- 100 g (3½ oz) cherry tomatoes, chopped into quarters
- bunch of basil, parsley or chives, roughly chopped
- plain flour, for dusting
- 250 g (8 oz) filo pastry, thawed if frozen
- pepper

**1** Sprinkle a few drops of the oil on to the baking sheet and ask your little one to smear it all over with their hands while you set the oven to 190°C (375°F), Gas Mark 5.

**2** Put the feta, tomatoes and herbs into a small bowl. Season with pepper and stir gently together.

**3** Ask your child to sprinkle a little flour over the work surface, then unroll the filo pastry on to it. Peel off 2 sheets and roll up the rest for later, keeping it moist under a damp tea towel. Place one sheet on top of the other and using a sharp knife cut both into 6 squares each measuring about 12 cm (5 inches).

**4** Show your child how to brush these squares with a little oil (pour the oil into a bowl) and then stack 3 squares on top of one another so that they make a 12-pointed star.

**5** Help them take a heaped teaspoon of the cheese mixture and place it in the middle of the squares.

**6** Now for the tricky bit. Pick up the edges of the squares and pinch them together to make a bag. It's easy once you get the hang of it but very little ones may need help.

**7** Place the parcel on the prepared baking sheet and repeat with the other squares of pastry until you have made 4 parcels. Then repeat with 2 more sheets of the pastry until you have used all the filling mixture.

**8** Bake for 5–10 minutes or until crisp and golden, then remove from the oven and allow to cool on the baking sheet.

**TINY TIP** Wrap up the leftover filo pastry sheets in clingfilm and keep them in the refrigerator until next time you make money bags.

**PLACE THE CHEESE MIXTURE** IN THE MIDDLE OF EACH SQUARE

# Garlic puffy bread

**MAKES** 1 x 35 cm (14 inch) circle of bread  **PREP TIME** 45 minutes, plus rising
**COOKING TIME** 10–15 minutes

### children love helping themselves to this lovely soft focaccia and it's surprisingly easy to make.

## Equipment

small mixing bowl • wooden spoon •
28 x 18 cm (11 x 7 inch) shallow
baking tin • kitchen paper • large
mixing bowl • clingfilm

## Ingredients

- 225 ml (7½ fl oz) pre-boiled
  warm water
- 2 teaspoons active dried yeast
- 1 teaspoon sugar
- 1 tablespoon olive oil
- 2 x 150 g (5 oz) packs pizza
  base mix
- plain flour, for dusting
- 2 garlic cloves, thinly sliced
- 1 teaspoon salt flakes

**1** Have your child put the warm water, yeast and sugar into a small mixing bowl. Stir together, then leave in a warm place for 15 minutes or until frothy on top.

**2** Meanwhile, pour a few drips of olive oil on to the baking tin and have your little one smear it all over with their hands or a piece of kitchen paper.

**3** Put the pizza base mix in a large mixing bowl and have your child add the yeast mixture and then stir it all together to make a soft dough.

**4** Sprinkle some flour on to the work surface, place the dough in the middle, then knead it for at least 5 minutes. Let your little one have a go at bashing it about but you will probably have to take over to knead the dough until it is elastic and smooth in texture. (See tips for kneading dough on page 10.)

**5** Place the dough into the prepared baking tin and help your child to press it into the corners. Scatter over the garlic slices and the salt.

**6** Smear some oil on to a piece of clingfilm and lay this over the top of the dough. Leave the dough in a warm place to rise for about 30 minutes or until it has doubled in height.

**7** Set the oven to 220°C (425°F), Gas Mark 7. Show your child how to make dimples all over the dough by gently pressing their fingers into it. Drizzle over the remainder of the olive oil, then bake for 10–15 minutes until golden brown.

**8** Carefully remove from the oven and allow to cool for at least 5 minutes before eating.

# Half-moon scones

**MAKES** about 14    **PREP TIME** 15 minutes    **COOKING TIME** 12–15 minutes

Scones are very easy and quick to make. They make brilliant snacks - try these spread with cream cheese and ham or warm with butter.

## Equipment

large baking sheet • sieve • large mixing bowl • wooden spoon • rolling pin • 6 cm (2½ inch) plain round or half-moon shaped cutter • pastry brush

## Ingredients

- cooking oil, for greasing
- 225 g (7½ oz) self-raising flour, plus extra for dusting
- pinch of salt
- 50 g (2 oz) cold butter, cut into small pieces
- 75 g (3 oz) Cheddar or your favourite cheese, grated
- 100 ml (3½ fl oz) milk
- 1 egg or 1 yolk, beaten, or milk, to glaze

**1** Sprinkle a few drops of cooking oil on the baking sheet and have your child smear it all over while you set the oven to 200°C (400°F), Gas Mark 6.

**2** Sift the flour and salt into a large mixing bowl. Add the butter and show your child how to rub the butter and flour together between their thumbs and fingers until the butter is broken up and covered with flour and the mixture resembles fine breadcrumbs.

**3** Stir in 50 g (2 oz) of the cheese, add the milk and mix with a wooden spoon. Then put your hands back into the mixture and gently bring it together into a ball of soft dough.

**4** Sprinkle flour onto the work surface and tip the dough into the middle. Gently roll the dough out until it is about 2.5 cm (1 inch) thick (it doesn't need much rolling).

**5** Help your child use the cutter to cut out shapes and place them on the prepared baking sheet. Brush with the beaten egg or some milk and sprinkle with the remaining cheese.

**6** Bake for 12–15 minutes or until firm and golden.

**TINY TIP** To have lovely light, crumbly scones the secret is not to handle the mixture any more than you have to. It's the opposite of bread, in fact, which you need to knead.

# Cheesy twists

**MAKES** about 15  **PREP TIME** 15 minutes  **COOKING TIME** 8–12 minutes

### These little cheese straws were my first culinary triumph as a child.

## Equipment

nonstick baking paper • scissors •
2 baking sheets • cheese grater •
large mixing bowl • sieve • wooden
spoon • rolling pin • sharp knife

## Ingredients

- 50 g (2 oz) Cheddar cheese
- 75 g (3 oz) self-raising flour,
  plus extra for dusting
- ½ teaspoon mustard powder
- 50 g (2 oz) cold butter, cut into
  small pieces
- 1 egg

**1** Set the oven to 220ºC (425ºF), Gas Mark 7, and cut pieces of baking paper to fit the 2 baking sheets.

**2** Help your child to grate the cheese into the mixing bowl, then rest the sieve on top of the bowl, add the flour and mustard powder and show how to tap the sides or shake the sieve so the ingredients fall through.

**3** Add the butter to the mix, then show your child how to get their hands into the bowl and rub the cheese, butter and flour together between their thumbs and fingers until the butter is broken up and covered in flour and the mixture looks like fine breadcrumbs.

**4** Separate the egg for your child into yolk and white. Add the yolk to the mixture and discard the white. Stir with a wooden spoon until you have a stiff dough.

**5** Sprinkle lots of flour over a work surface and put the dough in the middle. Children can easily shape this dough with their hands and roll it with a floured rolling pin until it is about 5 mm (¼ inch) thick.

**6** Take a sharp knife and cut the dough into long strips, about 1 cm (2½ inches) thick. Help your child pick up each strip carefully and twist it gently before laying it on one of the prepared baking sheets.

**7** Bake for 8–12 minutes until golden brown, then remove from the oven and allow to cool on the baking sheets.

# Sunshine cornbread

**MAKES** 12 squares  **PREP TIME** 15 minutes  **COOKING TIME** 20–25 minutes

A lovely soft, golden-yellow bread that's delicious warm or cold with butter. Great with soups, stews or cheese and pickles.

## Equipment

baking tin, 20 cm (8 inches) square • kitchen paper • sieve • 2 large mixing bowls • wooden or large metal spoon • fork or whisk • skewer • cooling rack • sharp knife

## Ingredients

- knob of butter or margarine, for greasing
- 200 g (7 oz) cornmeal (polenta)
- 225 g (8 oz) plain flour
- 1 tablepoon baking powder
- 1 teaspoon bicarbonate of soda
- 1 teaspoon salt
- 425 ml (¾ pint) natural yogurt
- 100 ml (3½ fl oz) milk
- 50 ml (2 fl oz) maple syrup or 50 g (2 oz) brown sugar
- 2 eggs
- 50 g (2 oz) butter, melted

**1** Set the oven to 180°C (350°F), Gas Mark 4. Let your child smear butter all over the baking tin, using their fingers or a piece of kitchen paper.

**2** Have them sift the cornmeal, flour, baking powder, bicarbonate of soda and salt into a large mixing bowl and mix them together.

**3** Place the yogurt, milk, maple syrup or brown sugar, eggs and melted butter into another mixing bowl and beat together with a fork or whisk.

**4** Pour the dry ingredients into the wet and ask your child to stir them all together, just enough to combine them into a batter, as over-stirring can make the cornbread tough.

**5** Help your child to tip the mixture into the prepared tin, then bake the cornbread for 20–25 minutes or until golden brown on top and a skewer poked into the middle comes out clean.

**6** Allow to cool a little in the tin, then tip out on to a cooling rack. When cool, cut into 12 squares and serve warm or cold.

# Courgette muffins

**MAKES** 12    **PREP TIME** 15 minutes    **COOKING TIME** 20–25 minutes

## Delicious savoury muffins that are very quick to make and simple enough for children to do all by themselves.

### Equipment

12 paper muffin cases • 12-cup muffin tin • large mixing bowl • sieve • wooden spoon • measuring jug • fork • dessertspoon • cooling rack

### Ingredients

- 175 g (6 oz) courgettes, grated
- 200 g (7 oz) Cheddar cheese, grated
- 250 g (8 oz) self-raising flour
- 1 teaspoon bicarbonate of soda
- ½ teaspoon salt
- 200 ml (7 fl oz) milk
- 1 egg
- 4 tablespoons olive oil

**1** Ask your child to place the paper cases in the muffin tin while you set the oven to 190°C (375°F), Gas Mark 5.

**2** Place the courgettes and cheese in the large mixing bowl, sift in the flour, bicarbonate of soda and salt and mix together.

**3** Put the milk, egg and olive oil in a measuring jug and mix together with a fork. Pour this mixture into the other ingredients and stir until just mixed. Use a dessertspoon to spoon the mixture into the muffin cases so that each is nearly full.

**4** Bake the muffins for 20–25 minutes or until risen, golden and firm to the touch. Leave to cool in the tin for at least 10 minutes, then transfer to a cooling rack. Eat hot or cold.

**CLEAN UP ANY SPILLS**
BEFORE YOU BAKE

# Festive Fun

# Little devils' cakes

MAKES 12  PREP TIME 15 minutes  COOKING TIME 10–15 minutes

## These cakes are devilishly chocolatey with little red horns.

### Equipment

12 paper cake cases • 12-cup bun tray • large mixing bowl • wooden spoon • sieve • dessertspoon • cooling rack • medium mixing bowl • tablespoon • teaspoon or palette knife

### Ingredients

- 100 g (3½ oz) butter or margarine, softened
- 100 g (3½ oz) caster sugar
- few drops of vanilla essence
- 2 eggs
- 100 g (3½ oz) self-raising flour
- 3 tablespoons cocoa powder
- 2 packs (250 g/18 oz) ready-made red fondant icing, to decorate
- 1 tablespoon pre-boiled warm water

**1** Show your child how to place the paper cases in the bun tray while you set the oven to 180°C (350°F), Gas Mark 4.

**2** Put the butter, sugar and vanilla essence in the large mixing bowl and help your child beat them together until creamy.

**3** Add the eggs and beat the mixture again, then sift in the flour and cocoa powder and stir them in. Have your child spoon the mixture into the cake cases with a dessertspoon so they are half full.

**4** Bake for 10–15 minutes or until risen and firm to the touch. Remove from the oven and allow to cool for a few minutes before transferring to a cooling rack and letting cool completely.

**5** Put 1½ blocks of fondant icing in a bowl, add about a tablespoon of pre-boiled warm water and stir until you have a thick but spreadable icing. When the cakes are cool, spread the icing over the tops with the back of a teaspoon or with a palette knife.

**6** Have your child take small pieces of the remaining fondant icing and roll them into devil's horns, then stick them into the wet icing on top of the cakes.

**USE SMALL PIECES OF ICING**
TO MAKE DEVIL'S HORNS

# Cobweb biscuits

**MAKES** 30  **PREP TIME** 30 minutes, plus chilling  **COOKING TIME** 8–10 minutes

## These scrummy cookies are what's known as refrigerator biscuits as the mixture is chilled until firm enough to slice very thinly.

## Equipment

large mixing bowl • sieve • wooden spoons • clingfilm or baking paper • nonstick baking paper • baking sheet • scissors • sharp knife • cooling rack • small mixing bowl • teaspoon

## Ingredients

- 275 g (9 oz) plain flour, plus extra for dusting
- 200 g (7 oz) cold butter, cut into small pieces
- 100 g (3½ oz) icing sugar
- 2 teaspoons vanilla essence

FOR THE ICING
- 125 g (4 oz) icing sugar
- 1 tablespoon pre-boiled warm water
- black icing pen, to decorate
- small spider sweets or cake decorations, to decorate

**1** Put the butter into a large mixing bowl, sift in the flour and show your child how to rub the butter into the flour with their fingertips, until the mixture resembles fine breadcrumbs. Stir in the icing sugar and vanilla essence and have your child squish the mixture together with their hands until it comes together into a ball.

**2** Tip the mixture out on to a floured work surface and ask your child to squidge it together with their hands and then shape and roll it into a long sausage shape. Wrap in clingfilm or baking paper and chill for at least an hour.

**3** Set the oven to 200°C (400°F), Gas Mark 6, and ask your child to cut out a sheet of nonstick baking paper to fit the baking sheet. Remove the clingfilm or baking paper from the dough and slice as thinly as possible. Place these slices on the prepared baking sheet.

**4** Bake for 8–10 minutes, or until the biscuits are a light golden brown. Leave to cool for 5 minutes, then transfer to a cooling rack to cool completely.

**5** Meanwhile, make the glacé icing by sifting the icing sugar into a bowl, then add the water and stir it in. Add more water drop by drop until you have a thick icing that coats the back of the spoon.

**6** When the biscuits are cool, use a teaspoon to coat each with white icing. ake the black icing pen and draw on a simple cobweb design. Draw or stick little spiders on to the webs, then allow to set before serving.

**WRAP UP THE DOUGH**
TO CHILL FOR AN HOUR

**SHAPE THE ICING**
USING YOUR FINGERS

# Pumpkin heads

**MAKES** 12   **PREP TIME** 30 minutes   **COOKING TIME** 10–15 minutes

## children will have great fun squishing the icing for this recipe and rolling the pumpkin heads.

### Equipment

12 paper cake cases • 12-cup bun tray • large mixing bowl • wooden spoon • sieve • dessertspoon • cooling rack

### Ingredients

- 100 g (3½ oz) butter or margarine, softened
- 100 g (3½ oz) caster sugar
- few drops of vanilla essence
- 2 eggs
- 100 g (3½ oz) self-raising flour

TO DECORATE

- 1 pack ready-to-roll coloured icing (contains 4 x 125 g (4 oz) packs in red, yellow, green and black)
- black icing pen (optional)

**1** Show your child how to place the paper cases in the bun tray while you set the oven to 180°C (350°F), Gas Mark 4.

**2** Put the butter, sugar and vanilla essence in the mixing bowl and help your child beat them together until creamy.

**3** Add the eggs and beat the mixture again, then sift in the flour and stir it in. Have your child spoon the mixture into the cake cases with a dessertspoon so they are half full.

**4** Bake for 10–15 minutes or until risen and golden. Remove from the oven and allow to cool for a few minutes before transferring to a cooling rack and letting cool completely.

**5** Take the red and the yellow icing out of their packs and ask your little one to squash them together with their hands until they are mixed to form orange.

**6** Pinch off a little piece of the green icing and shape into a ball, then flatten into a circle and gently push on to the top of a cake. Pinch off a bigger piece of the orange icing and ask your child to roll it into a ball. Place this on top of the green 'pumpkin patch'. Now pinch a tiny piece of green and roll into a stalk and push on to the top of the orange pumpkin. Also take tiny pinches of the black and use to make eyes and a crooked smile. Alternatively, if your child finds it easier, draw the face on to the pumpkin head with a black icing pen.

# Bonfire buns

**MAKES** 8 **PREP TIME** 10 minutes **COOKING TIME** 15 minutes

**Simple chocolate orange buns made by the easiest one-mixture method and decorated to look like mini bonfires.**

## Equipment

8 paper muffin cases • 8-cup muffin tin • sieve • food processor (or mixing bowl and wooden spoon) • dessertspoon •cooling rack • sharp knife • large serving plate • teaspoon

## Ingredients

- 175 g (6 oz) self-raising flour
- 25 g (1 oz) cocoa powder
- 100 g (3½ oz) butter, softened
- 100 g (3½ oz) caster sugar
- 2 eggs

FOR THE ICING

- 75 g (3 oz) butter, softened
- 200 g (7 oz) icing sugar, sifted
- few drops orange or yellow food colouring
- 2 tablespoons orange juice
- 2 x 150 g (5 oz) packs chocolate fingers, to decorate

**1** Ask your child to place 8 paper cases in the muffin tin while you set the oven to 180°C (350°F), Gas Mark 4.

**2** Sift the flour and cocoa powder into a food processor, add all the other ingredients and whiz until smooth and evenly mixed. Alternatively, mash together the butter and sugar in a mixing bowl until light and creamy, beat in the eggs one by one, then sift in the flour and cocoa powder and stir until evenly mixed.

**3** Help your child to spoon the mixture into the muffin cases so that they are each just over half full.

**4** Bake for 15 minutes or until risen and firm to the touch. Remove from the oven and leave to cool in the tin for 10 minutes before transferring to a cooling rack to cool completely.

**5** Meanwhile, clean the food processor or mixing bowl. Add the icing ingredients and whiz for a few seconds or stir until evenly mixed, smooth and creamy.

**6** Show your child how to peel the papers from the cool cakes, then take each bun and slice off the part that has risen above the top of the muffin case. Slice this top part into 2 pieces and turn the bun upside down on a serving plate so it sits on the cut edge.

**7** Help your child to spread a coating of icing around the sides and then put a blob on the top of each bun. Stick the 2 pieces of sliced-off cake back on the top of each bun.

**8** Show your child how to stick about 8 chocolate fingers vertically around the sides of each bun so that they look like a stack of bonfire wood.

# Hot cross buns

**MAKES** 10  **PREP TIME** 30 minutes, plus rising  **COOKING TIME** 15–25 minutes

### Making your own hot cross buns together is a lovely way to spend an Easter Saturday morning.

## Equipment

2 baking sheets • large mixing bowl •
wooden spoon • tea towel • knife •
pastry brush • cooling rack

## Ingredients

- cooking oil, for greasing
- 350 g (11½ oz) strong white flour,
  plus extra for dusting
- 3 g (½ a sachet) fast-action
  dried yeast
- 1 teaspoon salt
- ½ teaspoon mixed spice
- 1 teaspoon ground cinnamon
- 25 g (1 oz) mixed peel
- 25 g (1 oz) currants or raisins
- 1 tablespoon vegetable oil
- 200 ml (7 fl oz) pre-boiled
  warm water
- 75 ml (3 fl oz) milk

TO DECORATE

- 375 g (12 oz) pack ready-rolled
  shortcrust pastry, thawed if frozen
  and taken out of the refrigerator
  15 minutes before use (you will
  only need half the pack)
- 1 egg, beaten

**1** Sprinkle a few drops of cooking oil on to the baking sheets and have your child smear it all over with their fingers.

**2** Put the flour, yeast, salt, spices and dried fruit in the mixing bowl and have your child mix them all together with their hands.

**3** Add the vegetable oil, milk and water and mix everything together with the wooden spoon. Have your little one put their hands back into the bowl and draw the mixture together into a firm dough. If the mixture is too dry to come together, add more water. If it is too gooey and sticks to your hands, add flour.

**4** Sprinkle flour over the work surface and tip the dough on to it. Knead the dough for at least 5 minutes. (See tips for kneading dough on page 10.)

**5** Break the dough into 10 equal-sized pieces and knead into balls, then place on the prepared baking sheets. Leave plenty of space between the rolls as they will double in size.

**6** Cover the rolls with a clean tea towel, then leave in a warm place for 1 hour or until doubled in size.

**7** Unroll the pastry and cut into strips 1 cm (½ inch) wide. Have your child brush the buns with the beaten egg and then lay the pastry strips over them to form a cross. Trim the pastry and use the offcuts for the next bun until all the buns are decorated.

**8** Brush again with egg and bake for 15–25 minutes or until golden. Remove from the oven and leave to cool for a few minutes, then transfer to a cooling rack and allow to cool or eat warm.

# Easter nests

**MAKES** 12  **PREP TIME** 20 minutes  **COOKING TIME** 20 minutes

## Wonderfully simple, little oaty nests are filled with chocolate eggs for Easter.

### Equipment

12 paper cup cake cases • 12-cup bun tray • large saucepan • wooden spoon • dessertspoon • teaspoon

### Ingredients

- 75 g (3 oz) butter
- 50 g (2 oz) soft light brown sugar
- 1 tablespoon golden syrup or honey
- 125 g (4 oz) porridge oats
- mini sugar-coated chocolate eggs, to decorate

**1** Set the oven to 180°C (350°F), Gas Mark 4. Show your child how to place the paper cases in the cups of the bun tray.

**2** Help your child to measure out the butter, sugar and golden syrup or honey into a large saucepan.

**3** Place over a gentle heat on the hob and stir until melted together and just starting to bubble. Remove the pan from the heat and add the oats, then stir together until they are evenly covered.

**4** Use a dessertspoon to spoon the mixture into the paper cases so that they are nearly full.

**5** Bake for 15 minutes. Remove them from the oven for your child and leave to cool for 15 minutes, then help them to make a dip in the middle of each one with the tip of a teaspoon so that they look like little nests.

**6** Leave to finish cooling. When the nests are cool, ask your child to put a few mini eggs into each one to decorate, then peel off the paper cases to serve.

**PLACE A FEW EGGS**
IN EACH NEST

**ADD A TAIL**
TO EACH EASTER BUNNY

# Easter biscuits

**MAKES** 30 **PREP TIME** 30 minutes, plus chilling **COOKING TIME** 10–15 minutes

## This dough is quick to make and can be cut into whatever shapes you want, then decorated with imagination!

### Equipment

nonstick baking paper • scissors • 2 large baking sheets • large mixing bowl • wooden spoon or hand-held electric whisk • sieve • clingfilm • rolling pin • 1 large and 1 small bunny and/or chick-shaped cutters • cooling rack • 2 small mixing bowls • dessertspoon • teaspoon

### Ingredients

- 100 g (3½ oz) butter or margarine, softened
- 100 g (3½ oz) caster sugar
- 1 egg
- few drops of vanilla essence
- 250 g (8 oz) plain flour, plus extra for dusting

TO DECORATE

- 2 tablespoons pre-boiled warm water
- 250 g (8 oz) icing sugar

FOR THE CHICKS

- yellow food colouring
- small cake decorations or icing pens

FOR THE BUNNIES

- few white mini marshmallows or other bunny tail-like decorations

**1** Help your child to cut 2 large sheets of baking paper to cover the baking sheets.

**2** Place the butter and sugar in a large mixing bowl and help your child beat them until creamy with a wooden spoon or hand-held electric whisk.

**3** Crack the egg for your child and add with the vanilla essence. Mix again until smooth.

**4** Sift in the flour and stir to make a soft dough. Have your child use their hands to pull all the bits together into a ball. If the dough is very sticky, add a little more flour.

**5** Wrap the dough in clingfilm and chill it for 1 hour.

**6** Set the oven to 180°C (350°F), Gas Mark 4. Dust a work surface with flour and help your little one roll or press out the dough with their fingers until it is about 5 mm (¼ inch) thick.

**7** Show your child how to use the cutters to cut out bunnies and chicks and place them on the prepared baking sheets.

**8** Bake the biscuits for 10–15 minutes or until a pale golden colour, then transfer to a cooling rack and leave to cool.

**9** Make up the glacé icing by stirring the water into the icing sugar in one bowl. Transfer half the icing to the second bowl. Adding the colouring to one bowl drop by drop. Use a teaspoon to spread the white icing over the bunnies and the yellow icing over the chicks, then decorate with cake decorations and/or icing pens.

PLACE CHERRY PIECES
BETWEEN THE BALLS

# Christmas garlands

**MAKES** 6  **PREP TIME** 30 minutes  **COOKING TIME** 15 minutes

**These garlands are fun to make and very christmassy. Instead of eating them, they could be hung by ribbons from your tree.**

## Equipment

nonstick baking paper • scissors •
2 baking sheets • large mixing bowl •
sieve • wooden spoon • pastry brush
• cooling rack

## Ingredients

- 50 g (2 oz) butter
- 150 g (5 oz) plain flour
- 50 g (2 oz) caster sugar, plus
  a little extra for sprinkling
- finely grated rind of a small
  unwaxed lemon
- 1 egg, beaten
- pieces of angelica and glacé
  cherries, to decorate

**1** Help your child to cut out and line 2 baking sheets with the nonstick paper while you set the oven to 190°C (375°F), Gas Mark 5.

**2** Put the butter in a bowl, sift in the flour and show your little one how to rub the ingredients together between their thumbs and fingers until the mixture resembles fine breadcrumbs.

**3** Add the sugar and lemon rind and have your little one stir everything together with a wooden spoon. Add most of the egg and stir again until the mixture comes together, then have them put their hands in again and draw the dough together into a ball.

**4** Show your child how to pick off small pieces of dough and roll them into balls, each about the size of a cherry. Press 8 balls of the cookie dough together into a circle, then repeat to make a further 5 garlands. Place small pieces of glacé cherry or angelica between the balls.

**5** Bake for about 15 minutes until pale golden in colour.

**6** Just before the end of the cooking time, brush with the remainder of the egg and sprinkle with caster sugar, then return to the oven to finish cooking.

**7** Remove from the oven and allow to cool a little before transferring to a cooling rack.

# Meringue snowmen

**MAKES** 9–12 **PREP TIME** 20 minutes **COOKING TIME** 1½ hours or overnight

**Meringues are a great favourite of ours and with an electric whisk they're a cinch to make. Children will enjoy making the snowmen shapes and giving them faces and will relish eating them.**

## Equipment

nonstick baking paper • scissors • 2 baking sheets • small bowl • a very clean and dry hand-held electric whisk or hand whisk • large scrupulously clean mixing bowl • teaspoon • tablespoon

## Ingredients

• 3 egg whites
• 125 g (4 oz) caster sugar
TO DECORATE
• currants
• glacé cherries, cut into pieces
• mixed peel

**1** Set the oven to its lowest setting and help your child cut out 2 squares of nonstick baking paper to fit the baking sheets.

**2** Show your child how to separate the egg white from the yolk by cracking each egg in half over a bowl and carefully tipping the egg yolk from one half of the shell to the other while letting the white fall into the bowl below.

**3** Help them to whisk the egg whites in a mixing bowl with an electric or hand whisk until the egg whites form firm peaks and you can hold the bowl upside down without the mixture falling out. Add half the sugar and briefly whisk again, then add the rest of the sugar and whisk again but only enough to mix in the sugar and make a thick, glossy meringue mixture.

**4** Show your child how to use a teaspoon to place a meringue head on a prepared baking sheet and then use a tablespoon for the snowman's body. Repeat to make 9–12 snowmen. Use currants for their eyes, glacé cherry pieces for their mouths and give them buttons down their fronts with more currants or pieces of mixed peel.

**5** Bake the meringues for 1½ hours. For best results, put them in the oven for an hour and then turn it off, leaving the meringues in there for 3–4 hours or until the oven is completely cool. This can easily be done overnight. In the morning you will have perfectly crisp meringues.

**TINY TIP** To whisk up egg whites successfully, the bowl and whisk must be scrupulously clean and dry.

**SHOW HIM OFF**
BEFORE YOU EAT HIM UP!

**CRUSH THE CORNFLAKES**
WITH A ROLLING PIN

# Rudolph's Santa snacks

**MAKES** about 14   **PREP TIME** 15 minutes   **COOKING TIME** 15 minutes

**We have it on good authority that Rudolph likes to make these to keep Santa going through the most important night of the year.**

## Equipment

nonstick baking paper • scissors • baking sheet • plastic bag • rolling pin • plate • large mixing bowl • wooden spoon • sieve • cooling rack

## Ingredients

- 50 g (2 oz) cornflakes
- 100 g (3½ oz) butter or margarine, softened
- 75 g (3 oz) caster sugar
- 1 egg yolk
- few drops of vanilla essence
- 125 g (4 oz) self-raising flour
- 25 g (1 oz) cornflour
- 7 glacé cherries, sliced in half, to decorate

**1** Set the oven to 190°C (375°F), Gas Mark 5, and help your child to cut out a piece of baking paper to fit the baking sheet.

**2** Put the cornflakes in a plastic bag and have your child crush them with their hand or bash them with a rolling pin, then tip on to a plate and keep for later.

**3** Put the butter and sugar into the mixing bowl and help your little one cream them together with a wooden spoon until pale and fluffy.

**4** Add the egg yolk and vanilla essence and stir in. Place the sieve on top of the bowl, add the flour and cornflour and have your child knock them through by tapping or shaking the sieve, then stir them into the mix.

**5** Ask your child to wet their hands so that the mixture doesn't stick, then take walnut-sized amounts of the mixture and roll them into about 14 balls.

**6** Next, roll the balls in the cornflakes until covered. Place them on the prepared baking sheets, leaving plenty of space between each, and decorate the top of each one with half a glacé cherry.

**7** Bake the biscuits for 15 minutes or until a light golden brown, then remove from the oven and allow to cool a little before transferring to a cooling rack.

# Gingerbread house

**MAKES** 1  **PREP TIME** 45 minutes, plus chilling  **COOKING TIME** 15 minutes

## This house is fun to make, but very little ones will need help with the templates and with assembly.

. . . . . . . . . . . . . . . . . . . . . . . . . . . . . . . . . . . . . . . . . . . . . . . . . . . . . . . . . . . . . . . . . . . . . .

## Equipment

nonstick baking paper • scissors • baking sheet • large mixing bowl • wooden spoon or hand-held electric whisk • sieve • clingfilm • pencil • ruler • rolling pin • sharp knife • fish slice • small bowl • dessertspoon • piping bag

## Ingredients

- 100 g (3½ oz) butter or margarine, softened
- 100 g (3½ oz) caster sugar
- 1 egg
- few drops of vanilla essence
- 200 g (7 oz) self-raising flour, plus extra for dusting
- 1 tablespoon ground ginger

ICING
- 125 g (6 oz) icing sugar
- 1 tablespoon pre-boiled warm water
- icing pens (optional), to decorate
- sweets and Christmas cake decorations, to decorate

**1** Help your child to cut a large sheet of baking paper to cover the baking sheet, then follow steps 2–4 for the Gingerbread Royalty on page 46. Wrap the dough in clingfilm and chill it for 1 hour.

**2** Meanwhile, make the templates for the houses. Take a large sheet of baking paper and draw on it one 10 x 15 cm (4 x 6 inch) rectangle, two 10 x 7.5 cm (4 x 3 inch) rectangles and two triangles, each with two sides measuring 6 cm (2½ inches) and one side measuring 5 cm (2 inches). Cut out these shapes.

**3** Set the oven to 180°C (350°F), Gas Mark 4. Sprinkle the work surface with flour and roll the dough out so that it is about 5 mm (¼ inch) thick. Place the templates on the dough and cut around them with a sharp knife. Transfer each piece to a baking sheet with a fish slice. Bake for 15 minutes, then remove from the oven and allow to cool on the baking sheet.

**4** To make the glacé icing, sift the icing sugar into a bowl, then stir together with the water until you have a thick consistency.

**5** Spoon the icing into a piping bag and twist the top together down to the icing, then pipe the icing on to the house.

**6** Use the largest oblong biscuit as the base and use the 2 small oblongs to form a tent shape on top. Secure with lots of icing along the join (this will look like fallen snow) and allow to set. Pipe icing along the edges of the triangles and carefully insert one into each end of the tent to enclose.

**7** Use more icing, or an icing pen, and sweets to decorate the house with windows and a door. Let set.

# Index

## ACKNOWLEDGEMENTS

CONSULTANT PUBLISHER: Sarah Ford
EDITORIAL ASSISTANT: Meri Pentikäinen
DESIGN: Eoghan O'Brien and Clare Barber
PHOTOGRAPHER: Vanessa Davies
PROPS STYLIST: Marianne De Vries
HOME ECONOMIST: Becky Johnson
PRODUCTION CONTROLLER: Sarah-Jayne Johnson

Huge thank yous from the author to her mum,
Sally Johnson, for introducing her to the pleasures
of baking and for her enduring support and to her
daughter, Summer, for her enthusiastic recipe testing
and tasting. Also to Marcus, Tash, Leo and Lara for
all their generous help during the writing process.